The
West Highland White Terrier

An Owner's Guide To

A HAPPY HEALTHY PET

Howell Book House

Wiley Publishing, Inc.

Howell Book House

Published by Wiley Publishing, Inc., New York, NY
All rights reserved. No part of this book may be reproduced or transmitted in any form
or by any means, electronic or mechanical, including photocopying, recording, or by an
information storage and retrieval system, without permission in writing from the
Publisher.
No part of this publication may be reproduced, stored in a retrieval system or transmitted in any form or by any means, electronic, mechanical, photocopying, recording, scan-
ning or otherwise, except as permitted under Sections 107 or 108 of the 1976 United
States Copyright Act, without either the prior written permission of the Publisher, or
authorization through payment of the appropriate per-copy fee to the Copyright
Clearance Center, 222 Rosewood Drive, Danvers, MA 01923, (978) 750-8400, fax (978)
750-4744. Requests to the Publisher for permission should be addressed to the Legal
Department, Wiley Publishing, Inc., 10475 Crosspoint Blvd., Indianapolis, IN 46256,
(317) 572-3447, fax (317) 572-4447,
E-Mail: permcoordinator@wiley.com.
Trademarks: Wiley, the Wiley Publishing logo and Howell Book House are trademarks
or registered trademarks of Wiley Publishing, Inc., in the United States and other coun-
tries, and may not be used without written permission. All other trademarks are the
property of their respective owners. Wiley Publishing, Inc., is not associated with any
product or vendor mentioned in this book.
Limit of Liability/Disclaimer of Warranty: While the publisher and author have used
their best efforts in preparing this book, they make no representations or warranties
with respect to the accuracy or completeness of the contents of this book and specifically disclaim any implied warranties of merchantability or fitness for a particular purpose.
No warranty may be created or extended by sales representatives or written sales materials. The advice and strategies contained herein may not be suitable for your situation.
You should consult with a professional where appropriate. Neither the publisher nor
author shall be liable for any loss of profit or any other commercial damages, including
but not limited to special, incidental, consequential, or other damages.
For general information on our other products and services, please contact our
Customer Care Department within the U.S. at 800-762-2974, outside the U.S. at 317-572-
3993 or fax 317-572-4002.
Wiley also publishes its books in a variety of electronic formats. Some content that
appears in print may not be available in electronic books.

Library of Congress Cataloging-in-Publication Data
Weiss, Seymour N.
The West Highland white terrier : an owner's guide to happy, healthy pet / Seymour Weiss.
p. cm.

ISBN 0-87605-494-7

1. West Highland white terriers. I. Title.
SF429.W4W47 1996
636.7'55—dc20   96-20461
                              CIP
Manufactured in the United States of America
10 9 8 7 6 5

Series Director: Dominique DeVito
Series Assistant Director: Ariel Cannon
Book Design: Michele Laseau
Cover Design: Iris Jeromnimon
Illustration: Casey Price and Jeff Yesh
Photography:
Front cover photos: Adult, Faith Uridel; Puppy, Paulette Braun/Pets by Paulette
Back cover photo: Judith Strom
  Cheryl Primeau: 62
  Joan Balzarini: 96
  Mary Bloom: 2–3, 5, 10, 54, 57, 60, 96, 136, 145
  Paulette Braun/Pets by Paulette: 12, 19, 32–33, 34, 41, 52, 56, 67, 96
  Buckinghamhill American Cocker Spaniels: 148
  Sian Cox: 43, 134
  Judith Strom: 13, 20, 24, 35, 38, 40, 50, 65, 73, 96, 107, 110, 128, 130, 135, 137, 139, 140, 144,
  149, 150
  Faith Uridel: 8, 45
  Jean Wentworth: 7, 22, 23, 39, 90
  Dr. Ian Dunbar: 98, 101, 103, 111, 116–117, 122, 123, 127
  Dan Lyons: 96
  Cathy Merrithew: 129
  Liz Palika: 133
  Susan Rezy: 96–97
Production Team: Kathleen Caulfield, Vic Peterson, and John Carroll

Contents

Welcome
to the
World
of the

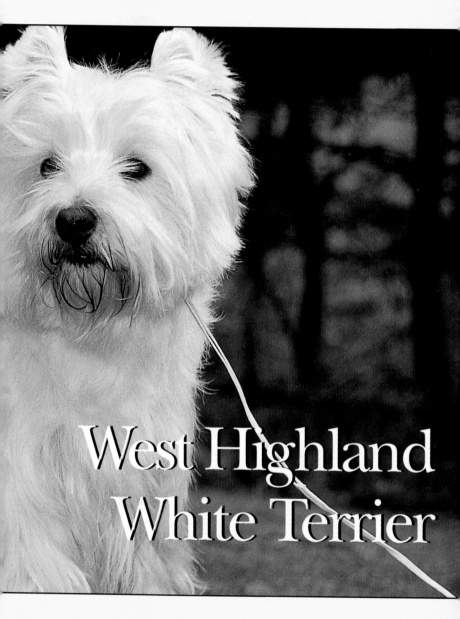

part one

West Highland White Terrier

External Features of the West Highland White Terrier

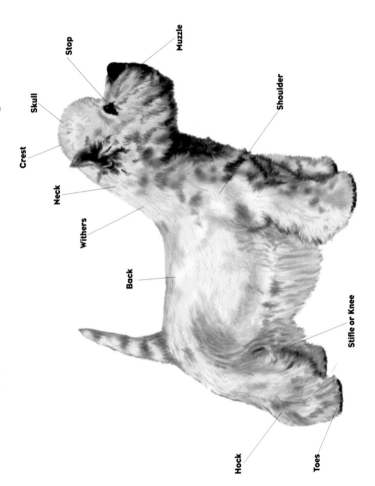

Muzzle

Stop

Skull

Crest

Shoulder

Neck

Withers

Back

Stifle or Knee

Hock

Toes

chapter 1

What
Is a
West Highland White Terrier?

The West Highland White Terrier is one of a group of small, active dogs originally developed to pursue and eliminate small animals that could make life uncomfortable around the homes and farmsteads of Scottish country folk. The breed's purpose in life made it essential for him to be sturdy and courageous, and to be equal to both a harsh environment and the fierce adversaries he was meant to exterminate.

The legacy of those early dogs is still present in the West Highland White today, and while we usually do not call upon our dogs to perform the breed's traditional work, we treasure the combination of physical and temperamental attributes that make this personable companion such a delight to those who know him best.

To fully understand and appreciate just what a Westie is, it is necessary to understand something of the breed's original function and how his conformation and temperament relate to what he was bred to do.

The Standard for the Westie

When the West Highland White became known to the world beyond heather and mist, his supporters wrote a word picture of the ideal specimen and used it as a guide for breeders and judges. Ultimately this word picture evolved into what fanciers call the *standard of the breed*. Every American Kennel Club (AKC) recognized breed has a standard. This standard describes in detail not only the breed's physical features but its temperament as well.

The standard for the West Highland White Terrier, in one version or another, has been used around the world for close to a century to define and describe the breed for all who love and care about the Westie. In the following discussion of the standard, the official standard appears in italics and the author's comments follow in regular type. For a copy of the complete standard, contact the West Highland White Terrier Club of America (see page 31 for the address).

> ## WHAT IS A BREED STANDARD?
>
> A breed standard—a detailed description of an individual breed—is meant to portray the *ideal* specimen of that breed. This includes ideal structure, temperament, gait, type—all aspects of the dog. Because the standard describes an ideal specimen, it isn't based on any particular dog. It is a concept against which judges compare actual dogs and breeders strive to produce dogs. At a dog show, the dog that wins is the one that comes closest, in the judge's opinion, to the standard for its breed. Breed standards are written by the breed parent clubs, the national organizations formed to oversee the well-being of the breed. They are voted on and approved by the members of the parent clubs.

GENERAL APPEARANCE

The West Highland White Terrier is a small, game, well-balanced, hardy looking terrier, exhibiting good showmanship, possessed with no small amount of self-esteem.

This section describes an attractive, no-nonsense working terrier. He must be of a size to "go to ground"—that is, small enough to fit into the dens and burrows of the animals he was meant to pursue.

He must also be "game"—brimming with courage and confidence, essential in a dog who was meant to tackle tough, determined prey. I have always liked the phrase "possessed with no small amount of self-esteem," for I believe this is the best thumbnail description of this little dog who casts a long shadow.

The Westie is an eager, confident terrier "possessed with no small amount of self-esteem."

Along with small size and gameness, the Westie should give the appearance of hardiness. He's a tough nut. Cold doesn't stop him, wet doesn't stop him, and obstacles don't stop him. Today's Westie is usually not called upon to work, but he should have the build and the heart to fill the breed's time-honored function. He exhibits in marked degree a combination of strength and activity.

SIZE, PROPORTION AND SUBSTANCE

The ideal size is between eleven inches at the withers for dogs and ten for bitches. The Westie is a compact dog, with good balance and substance. Short-coupled and well boned.

The Westie is a small dog who should be substantial enough to perform the breed's work with relative ease.

The breed standard is silent on the matter of weight, but specifies an ideal height of eleven inches for males (dogs) and ten inches for females (bitches), with a slight deviation being acceptable. The height is measured at the top of the shoulders (withers). A Westie should be short-coupled, which means that the body should be compact, with no obvious length. The Westie should also have sturdy bones so that you immediately get an impression of exceptional strength for a dog of this size.

HEAD

Shaped to present a round appearance from the front. Should be in proportion to the body. **Expression**—*Piercing, inquisitive, pert.*

A Westie's head is trimmed to give it a rounded shape.

The first thing most people will notice on a Westie is the head. Although the standard calls for a rounded appearance, this is achieved more through trimming than conformation. The head should also be in

pleasing proportion to the body, neither too small nor "pinheaded," nor too large and overdone. The expression is a combination of self-confidence and impish good humor.

Eyes

Widely set apart, medium in size, almond shaped, dark brown in color, deep set, sharp and intelligent.

There should be considerable space between the eyes on a good Westie head. Viewed head-on, the outer corner of the eyes should align approximately with the inner corner of the ears. The eyes are medium sized, almond shaped and dark brown. Sharp and intelligent, they look out from under heavy brows, producing a piercing look. The eye rims are black. Small, full or light-colored eyes are considered faulty according to the breed standard.

Ears

Small, carried tightly erectly, set wide apart, on the top outer edge of the skull. They terminate in a sharp point and must never be cropped.

The Westie's ears should be small, held tightly erect, and set wide apart on the top outer edge of the skull. If this is hard for you to visualize, think of the ears being placed at the corners of the head.

The ears should end in a sharp point, although some groomers prefer to take a tiny bit of hair from the very tip to make for a slightly rounded, more natural effect. Westie ears are always naturally erect and are never cropped. They are trimmed short, with the hair smooth and velvety, free of fringe at the tips.

Skull

Broad, slightly longer than the muzzle, not flat on top but slightly domed between the ears. **Muzzle**—*Blunt, slightly shorter than the skull, powerful and gradually tapering to the nose.*

A Westie's skull tapers gradually to the eyes. There is a definite indentation, called a stop, where the skull and the muzzle join. The skull is finished off with heavy eyebrows. A long or narrow skull is considered a fault.

The muzzle is blunt and slightly shorter than the skull. It should be powerful and taper gradually to the large, black nose. The jaws are level and powerful. Lips are black.

Bite—*The teeth are large for the size of the dog. A tight scissors bite with upper incisors slightly overlapping the lower incisors or level mouth is equally acceptable.*

Bite is important to any terrier. In Westies the teeth are surprisingly big, considering the small size of the dog. The bite should be either scissors (upper incisors slightly overlapping lowers) or level (incisors meeting tip to tip). Both types are equally acceptable. Defective or missing teeth are considered faulty, as are missing incisors or several missing premolars. Undershot or overshot mouths are also serious faults. These blemishes, however, have no bearing on a quality pet.

BODY

Neck—Muscular and well set on sloping shoulders. **Topline**—*Flat and level, both standing and moving.* **Body**— *Compact and of good substance.*

A Westie should have a muscular neck smoothly set on sloping shoulders. The neck is neither too short nor too long and should be in good proportion to the entire dog. The topline, which is the area of the

back from behind the shoulders to the base of the tail, is flat and level, standing and moving.

It is important for the Westie to have a compact, substantial body. The ribs are deep and well-arched in their upper half (extending at least to the elbow). The dog's sides should appear flattish or somewhat heart-shaped. The back ribs are of considerable depth, and the distance from the last rib to the upper thigh is as short as possible while still allowing free movement. The chest is very deep, and the loin is short, broad and strong.

The Westie should have a compact build that gives an impression of durability and strength.

TAIL

Relatively short, with good substance, and shaped like a carrot.

When the tail is held erect, it should never extend above the top of the skull. It is covered with short, hard hair with no fringe. The tail should be as straight as possible, carried gaily, but not curled over the back. Just as the Westie's ears are natural, the tail, too, is never docked.

FOREQUARTERS

Shoulders—Shoulder blades are well laid back and well knit at the backbone. Legs—Forelegs are muscular and well boned, relatively short but with sufficient length to set the dog up so as not to be too close to the ground. Feet—Forefeet are larger than the hind ones, are round, proportionate in size, strong, thickly padded.

A Westie's shoulders should be well-laid back, meaning that the tops point more to the base of the neck than further up the neck. The shoulders are well-knit at the backbone, meaning that the blades are close together at this point.

The Westie should have muscular forelegs with strong bones. The legs are relatively short, but long enough to set the dog up off the ground. The legs are reasonably straight and thickly covered with short, hard hair.

Feet are of great importance to a digging dog—they are the tools of his trade. A Westie's forefeet are noticeable larger than his hind feet, and are strong and tough looking. They may be turned out slightly. Dewclaws (the fifth digit) may be removed. Black pigmentation is most desirable on the pads of feet and nails, though black nails may fade as the dog ages.

HINDQUARTERS

Thighs are very muscular, well angulated, not set wide apart. Legs—Rear legs are muscular and relatively short and sinewy.

THE AMERICAN KENNEL CLUB

Familiarly referred to as "the AKC," the American Kennel Club is a nonprofit organization devoted to the advancement of purebred dogs. The AKC maintains a registry of recognized breeds and adopts and enforces rules for dog events including shows, obedience trials, field trials, hunting tests, lure coursing, herding, earthdog trials, agility and the Canine Good Citizen program. It is a club of clubs, established in 1884 and composed, today, of over 500 autonomous dog clubs throughout the United States. Each club is represented by a delegate; the delegates make up the legislative body of the AKC, voting on rules and electing directors. The American Kennel Club maintains the Stud Book, the record of every dog ever registered with the AKC, and publishes a variety of materials on purebred dogs, including a monthly magazine, books and numerous educational pamphlets. For more information, contact the AKC at the address listed in Chapter 13, "Resources," and look for the names of their publications in Chapter 12, "Recommended Reading."

Angulation refers to the degree of slope of a joint. The standard tells us a Westie's hindquarters should be

11

"well-angulated." The Westie's hock (which corresponds to our heel) should extend beyond the buttocks and be parallel to the ground when the dog stands naturally.

Dewclaws may be removed from the back feet as with the front feet, but it is very rare to encounter them.

COAT

Very important and seldom seen to perfection. Must be double-coated. The head is shaped by plucking the hair, to present the round appearance. The ideal coat is straight, hard and

white, but a hard coat which may have some wheaten is preferable to a white fluffy or soft coat.

The Westie's beautiful coat is a two-ply, or double, coat with a harsh outer layer and a softer undercoat. Both coats have a very specific purpose for the working terrier. The undercoat helps keep a dog warm and dry, while the outercoat protects the dog from brambles, rocky outcrops and, often, the teeth and claws of his prey. The only way to properly maintain a double coat is by plucking or stripping, usual for show dogs but rare in the case of pets. Maintained properly, the outercoat should be about two inches long. Today, however, there are very few correct, two-inch coats in evidence.

As a working terrier, the Westie needed his coarse, thick coat to protect him from the elements.

As the breed name indicates, the color is ideally pure white, but many dogs with very hard outercoats will show some wheaten (straw-colored) tipping. While not desirable, it is preferable to a white coat that is soft or fluffy.

Today, Westies trimmed for the show ring are very tailored and stylized. While some purists bemoan this development, there is no need for the pet dog to be so treated. Your Westie will be just fine if his body coat is trimmed to neatness, his legs, feet and ears are neatly tidied, and enough hair is left on the skull and around the head to act as a frame for the typical Westie expression.

GAIT

Free, straight and easy all around. It is a distinctive gait, not stilted, but powerful with reach and drive.

Bear the Westie's work in mind once more and visualize a physically sound animal than can get from point A to point B with no physical strain whatever. A Westie's movement, like every other component of the breed, should call attention to his physical ruggedness and happy outlook on life.

Though your pet Westie may not look exactly like the standard suggests, you'll enjoy him for his endearing personality!

TEMPERAMENT

Alert, gay, courageous and self-reliant, but friendly. **Faults—** *Excess timidity or excess pugnacity.*

Consider the fact that in Scotland, Westies were traditionally worked in packs. To have a dog without courage or one more focused on fighting with the dog alongside him than at getting the game would have been counter-productive and would not have been tolerated. What the early breeders did for you and me by creating a dog with balanced characteristics, was to give us an animal with unlimited terrier sparkle but not so fiery an attitude that owning the dog is a daily ordeal.

You will truly love your pet Westie for his wonderful personality. As you look for a puppy, keep that point foremost in your mind.

chapter 2

The
West Highland
White Terrier's
Ancestry

Ch. Wolvey Pattern of Edgerstoune (1942).

When considering the history of the West Highland White, it is important to remember that we are dealing in possibilities, probabilities and a few Celtic legends thrown in. In all likelihood the breed's earliest ancestor was a kind of generic Scotch Terrier. This ancestor probably most closely resembled the modern Cairn Terrier, but not that closely. Until the West Highland emerged as a distinct breed in the late nineteenth century, his ancestry is really a matter of conjecture.

The First Scottish Terriers

Several centuries ago in Scotland and its Western Isles, terrier-type dogs were bred specifically to hunt and exterminate vermin. To the owners of these dogs, form and style were of little importance unless they contributed specifically to the dogs' function. Size was variable, and coat color and markings were varied and random. Those dogs bore little resemblance to the cultivated terriers familiar to us today.

Over a long period of time, terriers began to branch into distinctly different breeds. Terrier owners bred for certain characteristics over others, and the breeds began to differentiate. But it was still quite a melting pot. A dog's ancestry was whatever the owner, farmer or gamekeeper said it was. There might have been several dozen terriers named "Jock" over a fifty-mile area. In those days, there was no accurate way of knowing who was who or what was what. You could never be sure whether a given dog was sired by MacDonald's Jock or Fraser's Jock or McPherson's Jock.

We do know from historical records that terriers from Scotland were known from the days of Queen Elizabeth I and King James I. The court physician for Queen Elizabeth, Johannes Cauius (John Keyes), wrote the first dog book ever to be translated into English, *Of Englishe Dogges*. The book mentions "terrars from the barbarous borders northward," or terriers from Scotland. King James made a gift of white terriers from Argyllshire, Scotland, to the king of France. Correspondence regarding the King's generosity indicates that the gift was greatly appreciated.

As the Westie developed into a distinct breed, it looked less and less like its cousin, the Cairn Terrier.

The Emergence of the Westie

While the working terriers of Scotland were known in all colors and combinations of colors, in some places white was considered a mark of impurity. It was the practice of some breeders to destroy white puppies at birth.

One legend describes how this distasteful practice came to a well-deserved end. After returning from service in the Crimean War, Col. E. D. Malcolm, a venerable soldier and sportsman, was out hunting fox on his estate Poltalloch in Argyllshire. In the excitement of the hunt, Col. Malcolm shot at what he thought was a fox. It was one of the Colonel's favorite Cairns. With the tragic accidental death of this dog, the Colonel vowed from that day forward to breed only the "white-uns." This is generally credited with being the genesis of the West Highland White Terrier.

Some hunters preferred the Westie's white coat because it made the dog easily distinguishable from the quarry.

As the separate breeds emerged, they began to look less and less alike. The Scottish Terrier became heavier, lower to the ground and more substantial, with larger bones. The Cairn was smaller and longer in body. He remained most faithful to the old identity. Even today the Cairn is the smallest of the highland terriers, with a longer, sinuous body and the physical make to hunt all manner of vermin in rocks, crevices and among the stoneheaps that gave the breed its name.

At the beginning of the twentieth century, some of the larger dog shows in England began to include classes for Westies, originally called Poltalloch Terriers.

At the Crufts show in London in 1907, West Highlands received their own classification under the name West Highland White Terrier for the first time.

But even as the Westie emerged as a distinct breed, there are documented records of breedings involving Westies and Cairn Terriers and, in some instances, even Scotties. This situation existed until 1917, when the American Kennel Club stepped in and took the position that any English Westie showing one or more Cairn ancestors in its pedigree in the first three generations was ineligible for registration in this country. Before long, the Kennel Club in England could only go along with American policy and do likewise. The two breeds have been distinct ever since.

The Westie in America

The Westie's first appearance in the show ring occurred in England, but Americans were quick to recognize the breed's numerous virtues. The breed was shown at Westminster in 1906 under the name Roseneath Terrier, and was first listed in the AKC studbook two years later under the same name. The breed name was ultimately changed to West Highland White Terrier on May 31, 1909, and has remained so ever since. The West Highland White Terrier Club of America came into being in September 1909 and continues as the primary protector of the breed's fortunes in this country.

WHERE DID DOGS COME FROM?

It can be argued that dogs were right there at man's side from the beginning of time. As soon as human beings began to document their own existence, the dog was among their drawings and inscriptions. Dogs were not just friends, they served a purpose: There were dogs to hunt birds, pull sleds, herd sheep, burrow after rats—even sit in laps! What your dog was originally bred to do influences the way it behaves. The American Kennel Club recognizes over 140 breeds, and there are hundreds more distinct breeds around the world. To make sense of the breeds, they are grouped according to their size or function. The AKC has seven groups:

1) Sporting, 2) Working,
3) Herding, 4) Hounds,
5) Terriers, 6) Toys,
7) Non-Sporting

Can you name a breed from each group? Here's some help: (1) Golden Retriever; (2) Doberman Pinscher; (3) Collie; (4) Beagle; (5) Scottish Terrier; (6) Maltese; and (7) Dalmatian. All modern domestic dogs (*Canis familiaris*) are related, however different they look, and are all descended from *Canis lupus*, the gray wolf.

*The Westie has
appeared on every-
thing from whiskey
bottles to great
works of art. Here
he is shown on
Player's cigarette
cards from 1938.*

From the time the Westie was first recognized by the AKC, and up to the year 1962, the breed maintained moderate numbers and a small loyal following of enthusiasts. Under ordinary circumstances that would not get a breed noticed when competing for attention with Cockers, Boxers and other popular, established breeds of earlier decades. But the Westie had a friend in the James Buchanan Distilling Company of Glasgow, Scotland. Buchanan was the distiller of Black & White Scotch Whisky and used a Scottish Terrier and a West Highland White in an international advertising campaign that got the Westie noticed. *Life* magazine regularly featured ads showing the playful pair in all kinds of mischief, to sell the popular brand of scotch.

PLAYER'S CIGARETTES

WEST HIGHLAND
WHITE TERRIER

Famous artists of the day were commissioned to execute imaginative renderings. Morgan Dennis, a famous American illustrator, was closely associated with the black-and-white dogs, and his original works are highly prized by today's collector. Even copies of the magazine ads are in brisk demand, with many being framed, matted and hung in the homes of fanciers.

Because of the Black & White initiative, Westie lovers have, over the years, owned and enjoyed a variety of appropriately decorated barware that has been manufactured to promote the whisky. Many are avid collectors with amazing "toys" to show off.

The Passion for Westie Collectibles

Numerous Westie enthusiasts are also avid collectors of Westie art objects. The Black & White articles just mentioned are but one part of all the truly beautiful Westie art available for the dedicated and sharp-eyed. Westies have captured the imaginations of many of the world's most celebrated artists and sculptors.

Probably the most famous Westie painting of all is *Dignity and Impudence,* by Sir Edwin Henry Landseer. This late-nineteenth-century work shows a Bloodhound and a Westie sitting together in a dog-house. If you have experience with Westies, you'll know which is dignity and which is impudence. If you are about to become acquainted with the Highlander, you'll find out very soon, I promise you. The original hangs in London's Tate Gallery and must be seen close up to be fully appreciated.

Other artists have immortalized the Westie as well. Arthur Wardle painted a beautiful double-head study titled *Jock and Jean.* John Emms painted an expressive work called *The Warrener's Pony.* It shows a Westie mother nursing her puppy while sitting along-side a pony loaded with the proceeds of a successful rabbit hunt.

The Westie's popularity soared in the United States after 1962.

Westie Popularity Grows

Over the years Westies made small, steady increases in popularity, but all that changed when a certain English Westie came to these shores in the late 1950s. His name was Elfinbrook Simon. Simon showed himself to be a first-class show dog and established himself as an important winner in a show career that is most conser-vative by today's standards. The high point of his career came in 1962 when Simon was Best-in-Show at the Westminster Kennel Club show in New York.

Simon was an electrifying showman and won the Garden in front of a TV audience of millions. After he was motioned to the winner's spot, he lifted his leg on the Best-in-Show sign and this brought the house down. No one ever forgot Westies after that "well-aimed" commentary.

In 1962 registrations jumped from 699 to 930. It was the biggest jump ever, and the Westie has never looked back. Now, more than thirty years later, the West Highland ranks in the upper one-fourth of all breeds registered with the AKC and is second among terrier breeds only to the Miniature Schnauzer.

Westies are intelligent, energetic dogs who can be trained to excel in a variety of competitive activities. This one is in an obedience trial.

A regular procession of dogs followed Simon into the winner's circle everywhere. The Westies on parade made the most of their opportunities to make more friends. The males showed their macho self-importance—hurling challenges at their rivals, marking their territories and scratching up the turf even at indoor shows! Over time this positive public image had a "trickle down" effect that resulted in the Westie's present popularity.

Activities You and Your Westie Can Do

Most Westies, even of the finest breeding, never venture into the show ring. However, there are lots of fun things you and your Westie can do together. You can try a little organized competition, or you can make your own fun. The limits are bounded only by your own imagination. See Chapter 9, "Getting Active with Your Dog" for more information on the activities discussed below.

WESTIES IN OBEDIENCE

Westies are quite good in obedience, and many have won a number of demanding titles in competition with all breeds. Whether you compete or not, remember to make training fun and interesting. Westies have nimble minds and need to be stimulated. A little legwork will help you find a local training class right in your community or not far away.

If, in the course of your training, you find that you and your dog like the work and function well as a team, you might want to look into obedience competition. The chances are excellent that the instructor can help you get started.

Make preliminary inquiries through your instructor or with the help of the West Highland White Terrier Club of America, whose name and address appear on page 31. The Club is very supportive of obedience and sponsors a large trial every October in conjunction with the club's national specialty show.

AGILITY

In canine agility, dogs must negotiate a series of obstacles—jumps, tunnels, poles—and they dearly love the excitement of this popular, fast-growing sport. If agility sounds like something you and your Westie would enjoy doing, talk to others who are involved. Your advisers need not be Westie people, but a number of Westie enthusiasts have tried agility and find it right up the breed's alley.

EARTHDOG TRIALS

Very recently the AKC has introduced a program into its series of performance events called earthdog trials. Obviously, this program is for small terriers and Dachshunds and is tailor-made for Westies. In earthdog trials, competitors are sent down a wooden tunnel at the end of which is a cage of rats. The object is to have the dogs go willingly into the tunnel, proceed quickly to the end and "give tongue" (bark) at the rats for a specified interval. There are a number of levels and titles available for competitors.

Earthdog trials are growing in popularity because they are exciting and give the dogs a chance to excel in a skill that is instinctive to them.

chapter 3

The **World**

According to the

West Highland
White Terrier

Before you make arrangements to visit a breeder, now is the ideal time to learn as much about Westies as you can. The purpose of this chapter is to give you the answers you need so that you will not have a shred of doubt about whether the Westie is really the dog you want.

The Word That Says it Best

What is it really like to live with a Westie? If any experienced Westie owner had to come up with a one-word answer to that question, the word would have to be *fun*. Westies approach life and the world with a happy, lighthearted attitude that is downright contagious. When there is a Westie in your home, life is bright for everyone the dog touches.

Remember that a Westie does not realize she weighs less than twenty pounds. As a result, a Westie often thinks of herself as equal to anything any dog is called upon to do. They are ideal pets for town, suburbs or country. Many Westies divide their time between city homes during the week and a getaway place in the country on weekends—and they adapt to both wonderfully well. To a Westie, the number-one priority is to be close to the people she loves best, so if you like to jog or take hikes in the country, your Westie will want in on the fun and she *will* be able to keep up.

And that's regardless of the season. A Westie in the snow is a sight to behold—running, jumping and rolling about in the drifts. When she is done being the *abominable snowdog,* she will be covered from head to toe with the cold, wet stuff and as happy as can be. When you see this, you won't be able to help smiling yourself and sharing your Westie's joy of living even though you are going to be the one to towel her dry!

One of the first Westies we bred had an interesting experience in the snow. One year we had entered this girl at the Westminster dog show, and that winter turned out to be a very severe one. On a really bad day, I put her in the yard to exercise and when she came up the backstairs to return to the kitchen, she slipped and fell off the top step to the side. It was about a five-foot drop to the ground, and I was sure she would be seriously injured. But the snow was very deep, and she just went in up to her neck, hind feet first. All that could be seen of her was a very surprised snow-white face accented by a black button nose and two dark eyes. The snow had completely broken her fall. When I realized that the only injury was to Violet's

The Westie is a fun, happy and energetic companion.

23

*Your Westie
loves to be
included in
whatever you
do; hikes in the
country are a
favorite activity.*

self-esteem, I was so relieved that I couldn't stop laughing. I waded into the snow to rescue the snow-bound beauty, brought her into the kitchen, dried her coat very thoroughly and she was as good as new.

Westies love a long walk or a safe run off-lead. Checking out all the delicious smells and chasing squirrels are all important Westie agenda items.

A Dog for the Whole Family

A Westie is a dog for the entire family. They can rough and tumble with the best of them and can be peaceful and quiet when called upon to be.

The Westie can stand up to the rowdy play of teenagers and usually understands how to behave around younger children. Many senior citizens own Westies and find them wonderful, understanding companions who bring a sunny outlook into lives that so need it. Many Westies owners use their pets as Therapy Dogs, visiting local hospitals and nursing homes.

WESTIES AND YOUNG CHILDREN

While the subject is well treated in Chapter 10, I feel it is important to post a warning about bringing a very young Westie into a home with a very young child. I make it a rule never to sell or recommend a Westie puppy to families with children under five years of age. A very young child will not understand that this irresistible thing is sensitive to pain, needs rest on a regular basis and must be handled gently at all times. The puppy will not understand that this small replica of the people she loves is not acting out of malice when a tail or ear gets pulled, a squeeze is too tight or an eye gets poked. Faced with these physical torments, a young Westie puppy will respond in the only way she knows how—by putting teeth into her side of the argument. I have yet to meet a parent willing to give up the baby and keep the puppy if things fail to go smoothly.

A True Terrier Personality

If you are considering a Westie pet, you must first like terriers or any dog with an active, get-up-and-go outlook on life. If your idea of a good pet is one who lies at your feet and is a passive presence in your life, a Westie would probably be a poor choice for you.

WESTIES DO BARK

People often speak disparagingly of "yappy little terriers," but what these critics fail to realize is that there were good reasons for Westies and related breeds to be vocal when they routinely did a terrier's work. The nature of the breed goes back to working requirements.

Any dog going to ground was required either to kill the quarry underground or alert the huntsman to the location of the prey so that it could be dug out and dispatched. Naturally the dog

---

A DOG'S SENSES

Sight: With their eyes located farther apart than ours, dogs can detect movement at a greater distance than we can, but they can't see as well up close. They can also see better in less light, but can't distinguish many colors.

Sound: Dogs can hear about four times better than we can, and they can hear high-pitched sounds especially well. Their ancestors, the wolves, howled to let other wolves know where they were; our dogs do the same, but they have a wider range of vocalizations, including barks, whimpers, moans and whines.

Smell: A dog's nose is his greatest sensory organ. His sense of smell is so great he can follow a trail that's weeks old, detect odors diluted to one-millionth the concentration we'd need to notice them, even sniff out a person under water!

Taste: Dogs have fewer taste buds than we do, so they're likelier to try anything—and usually do, which is why it's especially important for their owners to monitor their food intake. Dogs are omnivores, which means they eat meat as well as vegetable matter like grasses and weeds.

Touch: Dogs are social animals and love to be petted, groomed and played with.

would accomplish any required signaling by loud, persistent barking. To those hunters, the terrier with the big voice and the inclination to use it was considered a valuable addition to any hunting effort.

Most Westies are never used for work at the turn of the twenty-first century, but they are still equipped for their traditional calling, and that includes the use of their voice. It is a fact: Westies are vocal, some more than others, but a Westie needs little encouragement to express her own opinion about the affairs of her world. Of course, this means that a Westie is usually a very keen watchdog. Obviously, her size rules out her effectiveness as a guard dog (though not in her opinion), but that loud bark is often enough to discourage intruders.

Today a Westie's main concern is having fun, not chasing quarry.

The down side is that not everyone can be expected to understand or appreciate the reason for the breed's vocal nature. If you live in a high-rise apartment building and spend a good deal of your time out of your apartment, your Westie in these circumstances might bark from boredom or in response to every passing footstep. The result can be some unhappy neighbors and a sticky situation for you.

Training the noisy dog will improve matters. We hope your Westie will never exceed normal conversational levels, but it is wise to understand the potential problems of dealing with a canine "motor mouth."

EXERCISE REQUIREMENTS

Even though a Westie is small, she is active and loves being on the go. A Westie should have several good walks on-lead every day or access to a fenced yard.

A healthy adult Westie will do fine with three or four daily walks, at least one of which should be fairly long. Walking on a leash provides rhythmic exercise for your dog and is beneficial for you, too. Who knows, you may even get to meet other Westie enthusiasts on your way. It doesn't even have to be a nice day for a Westie to have a good exercise session. You may not appreciate a walk in snow or bracing cold, but Westies will like it just fine. Bundle up!

Your Westie will also love to have you throw a favorite toy for her to catch and bring back for another toss. It's great fun and a good way for your Westie to exercise, but you and your pet may come to a clash of wills on the matter of when the game should end.

Never, under any circumstances, should any Westie be allowed to run off-lead where she cannot be kept under control. This little dog is amazingly quick and can be off and away in the blink of an eye regardless of how well trained she is. The sight of a cat or another dog will trigger those dormant terrier instincts, and more than one free-running Westie has come to grief under the wheels of a passing car.

Playing with a favorite toy is a good way to exercise your Westie.

WESTIES DIG

We must also consider the terrier trait of digging. Digging is part of a terrier's job description. Westies, like most other terrier breeds, were meant to dig. In the days of Colonel Malcolm, digging meant unearthing foxes; today digging means unauthorized rearrangement of the juniper bushes.

It is possible to curtail the digging to a certain extent, but it cannot be doused altogether. For Westies having access to a fenced yard, measures must be undertaken to dogproof the yard. See Chapter 4, "Bringing Your West Highland White Terrier Home," for more information on puppy-proofing your home.

Westies with Other Pets

Just as barking and digging are natural actions for terriers, hunting and killing what they consider vermin are also second nature.

If you are adding a Westie puppy to your household and own a cat or two, it is sometimes best for the animals to arrange their own social hierarchy. If you are adding a kitten to a home with a Westie already in it, you should make introductions slowly and supervise them carefully.

If you are bringing a Westie into a home with small animal pets (for example, gerbils or hamsters), you should relocate these animals so that they are Westie-proof. A high shelf would do nicely.

Never make the mistake that the dog will understand the difference between the gerbils in the kids' room and the mice in the garage. The Westie has always been an earthdog, and the passion for the hunt is still strong with her. To prevent potential catastrophes, make the proper provisions ahead of time.

CHARACTERISTICS OF A WESTIE

Energetic

Hearty

Fun-Loving

Should not be kept with pet rodents

Affectionate

Adaptable

May be prone to skin problems

Bringing an Older Westie into Your Life

Nowhere is it written in stone that the Westie you acquire must be a puppy. It is often possible to find an older puppy or even an adult Westie who would make a wonderful companion. Breeders will often keep more than one puppy from a litter to see which will develop into the better specimen. When it becomes evident which "keeper" is the better of the two, the second choice might be offered for sale to a good home. By the same token, an adult dog, young enough to adjust well to a new home, might be available to

the right person. I can't stress strongly enough that these dogs are wonderful candidates for pets.

An older puppy or retired show dog often has a list of formidable advantages. Most of these dogs are thoroughly socialized. They are seasoned travelers and maintain their cool in just about any situation. They don't require the whole series of shots a young puppy must have and are not likely

to be as destructive as a curious puppy in a teething stage. And they are likely to be leash broken and have at least a bit of training. Of course, they'll need some time to adjust to your routine and to work on manners. Westies are sociable dogs and make adjustments quickly and smoothly when going to a new home.

Getting an older Westie can be just the right thing for those who don't want to train a rambunctious puppy.

Contact the West Highland White Terrier Club of America for the address of your local Westie club. The local club can give you the names of breeders in your area who might be able to help you find an older dog.

Many of these clubs also maintain a breed rescue system. When a Westie is found in dire straits or loses her home, she is "rescued" and made available for adoption to the right home. If you think you might be interested in a rescued Westie, speak to the rescue officer of the local breed club. Know the situation and what will be required of you. If it seems right for you, go for it. You'll be getting a wonderful pet and brightening an innocent life at the same time.

What Your Westie Can Mean to You

The world according to the Westie is a world of activity and a celebration of life. It's a world in which a small, rough-coated being gives her people the outer limits of her adoration. You can spend a long, frustrating day dealing with the cares of the world, but come home to your Westie and you'll soon be reminded of how wonderful your pet knows you to be. Just turn the key in the lock and your Westie will issue a fanfare of joyous barks that chase away, if only briefly, the worries of a larger world.

Perhaps that's the reason that once a person allows a Westie into his or her life, often as not another will soon follow. Like the potato chip ad that challenges us to eat just one, Westies give so much pleasure that many people imagine that if one is great, two must be terrific. Guess what? These folks are right. To the true Westie lover, no other breed fits the bill for a companion quite as well.

In the world we and our dogs share, however, many pets are left alone for long periods while their owners are at work. This need not be a problem. When my wife and I met, she had four dogs in a small apartment and had a full-time position in a large department store with work that often involved long hours. No problem. The dogs got on fine, and quality time was the order of the day when my wife and her Westie family could be together. So be there for your Westie as much as you can and you'll both get along just fine.

MORE INFORMATION ABOUT WEST HIGHLAND WHITE TERRIERS

NATIONAL BREED CLUB

West Highland White Terrier Club of America
33101 44th Avenue NW
Sandwood, WA 98292

BOOKS

Faherty, Ruth. *Westies from Head to Tail.* Loveland, CO: Alpine Publications, 1981.

Hands, Barbara. *All About the West Highland White Terrier.* London: Pelahm Books Ltd., 1987.

Marvin, John T. *The Complete West Highland White Terrier,* 4th ed. New York: Howell Book House, 1977.

Nicholas, Anna. *The Book of the West Highland White Terrier.* Neptune City, NJ: TFH Publications, 1993.

Sherman, Florence. *How to Raise and Train a West Highland White Terrier.* Neptune, NJ: TFH Publications, 1982.

Tattersall, Derek. *Westies Today.* New York: Howell Book House, 1992.

VIDEOS

American Kennel Club, *West Highland White Terriers.*

Living

with a

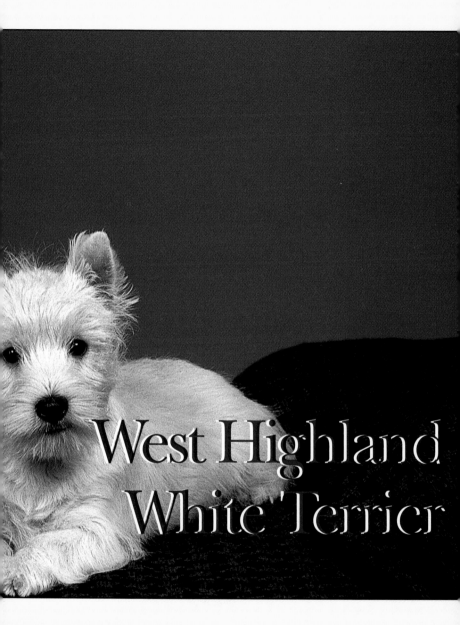

part two

West Highland White Terrier

chapter 4

Bringing Your
West Highland
White Terrier
Home

What an exciting time! You are about to bring your new Westie home. Considering the Westie's average longevity, you can expect some thirteen years of love and companionship from this dog.

Setting Up for Your Puppy

Before you bring your new puppy home, decide which spot in your home will be his special place. Like all dogs, Westies are social beings, so it's best if they have human company as much as possible. The spot you choose should be public enough to give your puppy the feeling of being a full part of family life, but out of the way enough so that he can rest as needed. The puppy's spot should be dry and draft-free, easily reached from any part of your home and easily cleaned.

You may want to look into a puppy playpen. This is an enclosure similar to a wire crate, but larger. It allows the puppy room to play, access to water, toys and food, and a "potty corner" if you want; it will keep puppy out of trouble with electric wires, chair legs and other favorite chewables. For Westies, even adults, two-by-three feet or three-by-three feet does nicely.

GETTING IT STRAIGHT ABOUT THE CRATE

It is good to see dog owners developing the right attitude about the place of a crate in the life of a pet dog. There was a time when many people were horrified at the suggestion that new puppy owners acquire crates for their pets. The thinking then was that this apparatus was a cage, representing cruelty and confinement. Actually, nothing could be further from the truth when a crate is used correctly. In a wild setting, canines make their home in a den. The den is where they sleep, eat, and bear and raise their young. It provides security and protection for them. In the same way, your puppy's crate is his safe haven in your home and beyond.

If introduced properly, your puppy's crate will be a safe haven from the busy world.

By feeding your puppy in his crate, you make the crate that much more attractive. Feeding the puppy in the crate also gives him a chance to have peaceful, uninterrupted meals.

It is a part of good planning to have a crate ready and waiting when you bring your puppy home. In fact, when you go to collect your puppy, bring the crate with you and have the puppy travel home in it.

A crate helps tremendously with housetraining. A healthy dog or puppy will usually not soil his sleeping place, so when you can't be with your puppy, keeping him crated until you can take him outside will help

35

avoid accidents and reprimands, and strengthen a growing puppy's physical control. It is not fair to expect a small puppy to refrain from answering the call of nature as needed (and for a puppy, that's often!), so you must establish a suitable timetable for taking your puppy out.

A crate is also the most effective protection for a dog in a vehicle. It acts as a seat belt for the dog, and also makes bringing the dog along safer and easier for the driver. Think about all the times you've seen dogs jumping back and forth in a moving car, or a driver holding a dog in his lap. Why invite catastrophe for your pet when normal driving is hazardous enough?

If you need to make a trip and take your dog with you, his crate will be his safe haven in a strange home or hotel room. If your dog needs to make an overnight stay with the veterinarian, his crate training will minimize any stress that a stay at the vet's may create.

Many styles of crates can be used successfully. I prefer the pressed fiberglass models often used by the airlines to transport pets. The correct size for a Westie is a #200. It is convenient to carry, easy to clean and not particularly expensive. Crates are also available in wire, wood and metal. They all have good and bad points, but the most important function they serve is proven safety for your Westie.

OTHER SUPPLIES

In preparation for your new Westie puppy, you will surely visit a store where pet supplies are sold. In some, the array of products can be truly dazzling, but it is good to remember that many are made to appeal to the owner rather than to be serviceable to the dog.

FOOD AND WATER BOWLS

I prefer good quality stainless steel bowls to any other products for the purpose. They last for years and can be cleaned easily. One of my bowls is more than thirty-five years old and has long outlasted the dog for whom it was originally purchased. In use just about every day, it looks the same as it did on the day I bought it.

Crocks are very popular as food or water bowls for dogs. I keep a very large water crock in my kitchen. When the vessel is heavy enough, dogs tend not to try tipping over their water supply. The disadvantage to crocks for feeding is their vulnerability to cracks. Plastic or lightweight metal bowls tend not to stand up to regular use. It's better to buy quality utensils at the beginning than to keep replacing bargain supplies that are really not bargains at all.

"MY KINGDOM FOR A TOY"

No doubt about it, Westies adore toys. We save the cores from rolls of toilet tissue and paper towels for very young puppies. They have a wonderful time chewing on them and tossing them about. The puppies can't hurt themselves with such items, and at the price, they can't be beat!

Toys with squeakers can be dangerous, as the puppy can remove the squeaker and swallow it. Latex pieces that are torn off toys can usually pass through a puppy's system without incident, but, again, the squeaker can cause choking or worse if swallowed.

Many dogs like chewing on rawhide, but rawhide has some disadvantages. Small pieces torn off and swallowed can cause intestinal blockage. If you give your Westie rawhide, watch carefully and remove the rawhide when it gets close to a swallowable size. In recent years, meat packers have been offering cow hooves and pigs' ears as safe chew items for dogs. The products are said to be 100 percent protein and completely safe for dogs. By the way, the dogs love them.

COLLAR AND LEAD

At one time, I always used plain, rolled leather collars and a four-foot-long leather leash with a good strong clip for walking my dogs. Those items are still excellent, but now you can get a nylon collar or a web collar

**PUPPY
ESSENTIALS**

Your new
puppy will
need:

food bowl

water bowl

collar

leash

I.D. tag

bed

crate

toys

grooming
supplies

and matching lead in any one of a rainbow of brilliant colors. Like the rolled leather collars, these do not wear down the hair around a dog's neck and the leash is easy on your hands.

Westies do not need choke-chain collars, and they should not wear harnesses. A harness encourages pulling, and a Westie just doesn't need to wear such an item.

DOG BEDS

Dog beds come in a variety of styles and are very attractive, but they are subject to damage from chewing. Westies grow big teeth and can do some serious chewing as soon as their second teeth come in. Their potential for chewing up all that wickerwork is formidable, but of greater concern is the potential of the wicker to slice up your puppy's internal organs. You can spray bitter apple on the bed, but it's still risky. Better to use a crate for your puppy than make a painful mistake. Wait till your Westie is grown and beyond the chewing phase to give him one. In the meanwhile, put some soft bedding into your puppy's crate to make him feel cozy and comfortable.

Your puppy will be delighted with a rawhide chew stick, but make sure he doesn't swallow sharp, small pieces.

Puppy-Proofing Your Home

Provide a safe environment for your Westie. A good rule of thumb when you are preparing your home for a new puppy is to take the same precautions you would for an active toddler. Keep electrical cords taped up out of the puppy's reach. Make sure you stow all household cleaners, detergents, paints, lawn products, medicines and any other potentially dangerous chemicals securely away. If you have a fenced yard, remember that Westies are excellent diggers, so you might want to sink some wire around the perimeter of the yard to discourage an escape attempt. Failing that, you might consider fencing off a small part of your yard as an exercise area.

Curious Westie puppies will chew on anything, so make sure that unsafe objects and substances are out of reach.

Bringing Your Westie Puppy Home

When your new puppy first arrives home, give him the opportunity to rest, especially if your trip home has been a long one. The puppy will need to relieve himself and will definitely need some quiet time. Many well-meaning new owners, in the excitement of the moment, show the new puppy to all the neighbors and their children's friends. This is the wrong thing to do. A puppy is a baby and doesn't know what to make of this strange place and these strange people. It's much better to give the puppy the chance to rest up and then inspect a small portion of his new surroundings. It won't take long for the characteristic Westie self-confidence to kick in, but treating the puppy properly at the beginning is essential to get your relationship off on the right track.

THE FIRST NIGHT

When you bring your puppy home, give him lots of love and attention but also be sure he has plenty of time to rest.

Some puppies will cry during the night for the first night or so, but it's just a symptom of homesickness and uncertainty. If your puppy does cry at night, don't go to him to comfort him. You will be letting the puppy know that it is okay to do this and encouraging the development of an undesirable habit. Do your best to ignore the crying if it happens. You may want to keep the puppy's crate in your bedroom for the sake of a night's sleep. If he starts to cry, just put your hand on the crate reassuringly, but don't take him out. Try to get something that has the smell of the puppy's first

home on it and place this in the crate. You may also want to get a ticking alarm clock. Wrap it in a towel and place it in the puppy's crate. This supposedly simulates the mother's heartbeat and may help to calm the puppy.

Establish a Routine

If you always remember that dogs are creatures of habit, you will be able to establish a good routine that your Westie will be happy with and you can handle easily.

Rigid adherence to a schedule is not realistically possible, but the routine should be followed as closely as possible. Put your puppy in the yard or walk him at the same times every day. Feed your Westie puppy at the same times every day and use the same food or combination of food.

LEAVING YOUR PUPPY ALONE

Eventually, you will have to leave your puppy alone. Reassure the puppy that you will not be gone long, and leave a radio on during your absence. The music and human voices will help keep your puppy reassured while you are away from him. If you will be gone for only a short while—say, no more than about two hours—you can safely confine the puppy to his crate. For longer absences, use a playpen or confine the puppy to a small area with an easily cleaned floor. If you decide to use a bathroom or laundry room, you are well-served to use an expandable baby gate across the door and get items such as towels or scatter rugs out of harm's way. Keep the crate in the room with the puppy, with the door open. If you leave him a towel, toys and a small imitation sheepskin rug, the puppy will have plenty to occupy himself with.

Identification

Make sure you provide your dog with some sort of identification. Even if you always walk him on a leash or keep him in a closed yard, accidents can happen. If your Westie does get away from you somehow, maximize the chances that you will be reunited by having your dog properly identified.

You and your new Westie puppy are on the brink of a wonderful adventure!

Keep some sort of **ID tag** on your Westie's collar. Whether it's a license tag from your town or a personalized name tag you've had made specially, some sort of identification on your dog's collar is necessary. If someone finds your dog, this may the only place he or she checks for identification, and it is certainly the easiest to interpret.

For some time now, people have been using **tattoos** as a means of tracing their dogs in the event of a loss or theft. A tattoo is a permanent marking and is usually made inside a dog's hind leg. If you wish to have your pet tattooed, ask your veterinarian for the name and address of someone in your town who does this. Your local dog trainer or kennel club member may also

41

know where tattoos can be done. The advantage of the tattoo is that it cannot be lost or removed. Your Westie may pull off his collar and thus his ID tag, or the tag may fall off the collar. A tattoo, on the other hand, isn't going anywhere.

The latest identification device is the **microchip.** A tiny chip is injected between a dog's shoulder blades and can be read with a special scanner. Unlike tattooing, there is no outward indication that the animal is identified in any way, and the scanners necessary to read the microchip are not yet widely available.

Congratulations

You and your new Westie puppy are on the brink of a wonderful life adventure. Your puppy is ready to give his all for you, and you must be ready to do everything you can to ensure that he lives a long, happy life. If you have any questions at all, check with the breeder who sold you your puppy, your veterinarian or a dog trainer in your local area who has had experience with Westies.

You will soon learn how bright your new Westie friend really is and will come to appreciate the rich dimension he adds to your life. Take the good advice of your dog's breeder and your vet, and have confidence in your ability to provide all that your Westie needs. You are about to have a wonderful experience that you will always remember.

HOUSEHOLD DANGERS

Curious puppies and inquisitive dogs get into trouble not because they are bad, but simply because they want to investigate the world around them. It's our job to protect our dogs from harmful substances, like the following:

IN THE HOUSE

cleaners, especially pine oil

perfumes, colognes, aftershaves

medications, vitamins

office and craft supplies

electric cords

chicken or turkey bones

chocolate

some house and garden plants, like ivy, oleander and poinsettia

IN THE GARAGE

antifreeze

garden supplies, like snail and slug bait, pesticides, fertilizers, mouse and rat poisons

---

chapter 5

Feeding
Your
West Highland
White Terrier

The importance of good feeding is obvious, but the rules for maintaining a dog on good food and a sensible feeding regimen are wonderfully simple. It is when dog owners start making up their own rules about feeding that good husbandry can become derailed.

Dog owners take their pets to the veterinarian when they become ill, to the groomer for a special occasion, or to a training session when the spirit moves them. However, they feed their pets every single day. What they are fed, when they are fed and how they are fed are of great importance.

Over the course of a dog's life, her nutritional requirements will change just as ours do, and it is important to be aware of those needs ahead of time. If you approach the entire matter of feeding from a commonsense point of view and arm yourself with good information, you can expect that your dog will be properly fed for her entire life.

TYPES OF FOODS/TREATS

There are three types of commercially available dog food—dry, canned and semimoist—and a huge assortment of treats (lucky dogs!) to feed your dog. Which should you choose?

Dry and canned foods contain similar ingredients. The primary difference between them is their moisture content. The moisture is not just water. It's blood and broth, too, the very things that dogs adore. So while canned food is more palatable, dry food is more economical, convenient and effective in controlling tartar buildup. Most owners feed a 25% canned/75% dry diet to give their dogs the benefit of both. Just be sure your dog is getting the nutrition he needs (you and your veterinarian can determine this).

Semimoist foods have the flavor dogs love and the convenience owners want. However, they tend to contain excessive amounts of artificial colors and preservatives.

Dog treats come in every size, shape and flavor imaginable, from organic cookies shaped like postmen to beefy chew sticks. Dogs seem to love them all, so enjoy the variety. Just be sure not to overindulge your dog. Factor treats into her regular meal sizes.

Feeding Your Westie Puppy

If you are about to get your first West Highland, you will surely want to know just what to do to make sure you feed her properly. Before you bring her home, ask what she is being fed and when, and stick to the same food and routine after you get her home. Do this for at least the first week or so.

In most cases, the puppy you get will be on three meals a day. Stick to this number of feedings as much as possible. A Westie puppy will continue to grow until she is about nine months old, and it is important to feed with this fact in mind. You may need to change feeding times to accommodate your own lifestyle. No problem. Just make sure that you ease the puppy into your requirements. Making abrupt changes can be stressful and physically upsetting for the puppy.

The three-meals-a-day routine should be followed until the puppy reaches about six months of age. At this point, put her on a morning and an evening meal until she reaches her first birthday. At a year of age, she will do well on one meal a day, with biscuits in the morning and at bedtime. However, if you prefer to keep your Westie on two meals a day, there is no reason not to. If you give her two meals a day, do not offer a morning biscuit.

What to Feed Your Westie

Today, we and our dogs benefit from extensive research that has been conducted to find the best foods available for routine, day-to-day feeding, as well as foods for growing puppies, geriatrics, dogs with specific health needs and dogs with high levels of activity. The various dog food companies have gone to considerable expense to develop nutritionally complete, correctly balanced diets for all dogs. Feeding the right amount of a high-quality food should suffice. That may, however, be easier said than done, as owners often have an emotional tendency to enhance their pets' food, often to the detriment of the dog (more on this subject later in the chapter).

Puppies and adults have different nutritional needs. Feed what's appropriate for each dog's age and activity level.

DRY FOOD (KIBBLE)

The basis of your dog's diet should be dry kibble. A high-quality, well-balanced kibble is nutritionally complete and will be relished by your dog under all normal conditions. Most major dog food companies manufacture a special formulation to meet the explosive growth of young puppies. These are highly recommended for daily feeding up to your Westie's first birthday. Use the puppy foods. They work! For a mature dog, choose a kibble with a minimum of 20 percent protein. This and other important nutritional information will be on the label.

Many experienced dog keepers are firm believers in feeding dry kibble, or just flavoring it slightly with broth or canned meat to heighten palatability. Others, just as adamantly, insist that the dog is a natural meat eater and her diet should contain significant amounts of fresh or canned meat. Actually, a diet that mixes both meat and kibble is likely to provide your dog with the best features of both foods. If one had to come down on the side of one food or the other, the winner would have to be an all-kibble diet. Studies have shown that dogs raised on all-meat diets often suffer from malnutrition and serious deficiencies.

ADDING CANNED FOOD OR MEAT

If you decide to add meat to the food, the best choice is beef. It may be freshly cooked, if you like, or canned. There are some very fine canned meats available, and it is a good idea for you to check the label, looking for about 10 percent protein. Chicken is also a good food source and is available in canned form. If you cook any poultry for your Westie, bone it carefully. The same is true for fish, which most dogs relish. Cottage cheese is another good protein source, especially for puppies or dogs convalescing from illness.

If you feed kibble with or without meat, add enough water to give the food a hashlike texture. It's better to add too little water than too much. Dogs generally do not like sloppy-textured food.

WATER

Besides feeding a high-quality food, you must keep ample clean, fresh water available for your dog at all times. It is vital to do so.

Establishing a Feeding Schedule

Establishing a feeding schedule depends on the demands of your own daily routine. Whatever time you decide, feed at the same time every day. Dogs are creatures of habit and are happiest when maintained on a specific schedule. Of course there will be days when you can't be there to feed your pet at her regular dinner hour. It's okay. An occasional break in the routine is not a disaster, as long as your dog knows that most of the time she will be fed at a set time.

How Much to Feed Your Westie

The amount of food you feed your Westie depends on the individual dog: her age, health, stage of life and activity level. If your Westie is very active, she will burn more calories and need more food than a house pet who doesn't get extraordinary amounts of exercise. There will be a difference in the eating patterns of a growing puppy and an elderly animal. If your dog is ill or convalescing, her food needs will also differ from the requirements of a healthy animal. Use your own educated judgment.

If a healthy dog cleans her bowl but still appears hungry, she might need a little more to reach the right amount of daily ration. Adjust accordingly.

Another way to determine whether you are feeding the right amount of food is to let the dog's condition tell you. If your dog is healthy but appears thin, you may want to feed a bit more. If the dog looks to be on the plump side, a more restricted diet may be in order. If you can't feel your dog's ribs beneath her fur,

HOW TO READ THE DOG FOOD LABEL

With so many choices on the market, how can you be sure you are feeding the right food for your dog? The information is all there on the label—if you know what you're looking for.

Look for the nutritional claim right up top. Is the food "100% nutritionally complete"? If so, it's for nearly all life stages; "growth and maintenance," on the other hand, is for early development; puppy foods are marked as such, as are foods for senior dogs.

Ingredients are listed in descending order by weight. The first three or four ingredients will tell you the bulk of what the food contains. Look for the highest-quality ingredients, like meats and grains, to be among them.

The Guaranteed Analysis tells you what levels of protein, fat, fiber and moisture are in the food, in that order. While these numbers are meaningful, they won't tell you much about the quality of the food. Nutritional value is in the dry matter, not the moisture content.

In many ways, seeing is believing. If your dog has bright eyes, a shiny coat, a good appetite and a good energy level, chances are his diet's fine. Your dog's breeder and your veterinarian are good sources of advice if you're still confused.

she's overweight. Get your vet's advice and start her on a diet.

The Picky Eater

A healthy dog will eat food when it's offered and most of the time will clean the dish. If you know your Westie is healthy, but she consistently refuses to eat the good food you put in front of her, don't get into the habit of pampering her by offering alternative foods. This will only stiffen her resolve to be more difficult. Feed her at the same time and in the same quiet place every day. Leave the food down for twenty minutes and then remove it entirely, whether she has eaten or not. Don't worry, a healthy dog will eat before she starves.

HOW MANY MEALS A DAY?

Individual dogs vary in how much they should eat to maintain a desired body weight—not too fat, but not too thin. Puppies need several meals a day, while older dogs may need only one. Determine how much food keeps your adult dog looking and feeling her best. Then decide how many meals you want to feed with that amount. Like us, most dogs love to eat, and offering two meals a day is more enjoyable for them. If you're worried about overfeeding, make sure you measure correctly and abstain from adding tidbits to the meals.

Whether you feed one or two meals, only leave your dog's food out for the amount of time it takes her to eat it—10 minutes, for example. Freefeeding (when food is available any time) and leisurely meals encourage picky eating. Don't worry if your dog doesn't finish all her dinner in the allotted time. She'll learn she should.

Feeding Two or More Dogs

If you have to feed two or more dogs, crates can be useful. In multiple-dog households, each dog should eat in her own crate—with the door locked. In this way, each dog will eat in comfort, without being threatened by another dog in the household. In the absence of separate crates, dogs should be fed where others in the home cannot get at their food.

Supplements—Do You Really Need Them?

Many owners believe that in a properly balanced diet, extra supplements are not necessary and might even lead to imbalanced diets in some cases. Pet owners rarely face situations in which extra supplementation is needed. Therefore, if you are feeding the high-quality food currently available, you probably do not have to add supplements to your Westie's diet. Ask your veterinarian for more information on determining a healthy, complete diet for your Westie.

People Food

When it comes to feeding a dog well, people often get caught up in their own perceptions about what's good and what's not. As a result, they end up feeding their dogs very poorly. That's because what may be a wonderful food for people can be a dreadful choice for your dog. Spicy food, junk food, rich sauces and so on are not good for dogs, however well-intentioned you are.

It can be okay to offer human food at times and to add table scraps occasionally to your dog's food, but do it wisely and in moderation. Dogs like carrots, broccoli and other fresh vegetables; some even like fruits. These are okay, as are bits of cooked meat (no bones). And remember all those balanced rations I mentioned earlier in this chapter: Quality food made specifically for dog feeding will do a better job of nourishing your pet than treats you may feel good about offering.

Never Give Your Dog Chocolate

Recently it has been found that chocolate in large enough concentrations can be lethal to your dog, so never give your dog this universally loved sweet. Your dog doesn't need it, can only be hurt by it and will never miss it. Never let anyone else offer her chocolate either. Your dog can't be expected to know how dangerous chocolate can be; it's up to you to monitor her diet and keep her safe.

Bones

On the matter of bones, your Westie is infinitely better off without them. Certain beef bones are safe enough, but others such as poultry, chop or fish bones are definitely dangerous and should never be offered. If you need another reason to keep bones away from your Westie, think of what a greasy mess a Westie who has been playing with a big soup bone can become. If you can't visualize it, trust me—it's not pretty, and there are many safe chewing items you can give your Westie that she will enjoy every bit as much.

While an occasional treat is fine, high-quality commercial dog food is the best possible diet for your dog.

Special Diets for Special Needs

Earlier in this chapter, I mentioned special diets available for dogs. These are usually available through your veterinarian and include low-sodium diets, diets for dogs with kidney and intestinal problems, as well as diets for dogs with food allergies. One of the most popular of prescription diets is the reducing diet. I have used these as needed and have found them not only effective but easy to use. And the dogs find them readily palatable.

If your Westie looks as though she has been living *too well*, you might want to ask your veterinarian about trying a prescription reducing diet or you might want to cut back on her regular food and substitute carrot strips for biscuits. If you have been in the habit of slipping her tidbits on a regular basis, stop now. Allowing a dog to become obese not only reduces her quality of life, it reduces her life, period.

FOOD ALLERGIES

Westies are no strangers to skin problems. This is a fact that cannot be denied and will not go away. Usually, there is no way to predict whether a young puppy will develop skin problems. When these skin difficulties are traced to a food problem, they can be controlled with diet. Consult your veterinarian for more information about how to handle this.

Many Westies who suffer from food allergies respond well when they are put on a soy-free dry food. Others will do nicely on a natural ration of lamb and rice. We know of one puppy with severe food allergies who does well on a diet of fish and potatoes with kibble made from these same ingredients.

TO SUPPLEMENT OR NOT TO SUPPLEMENT?

If you're feeding your dog a diet that's correct for her developmental stage and she's alert, healthy-looking and neither over- nor underweight, you don't need to add supplements. These include table scraps as well as vitamins and minerals. In fact, a growing puppy is in danger of developing musculoskeletal disorders by oversupplementation. If you have any concerns about the nutritional quality of the food you're feeding, discuss them with your veterinarian.

chapter 6

Grooming
Your
West Highland
White Terrier

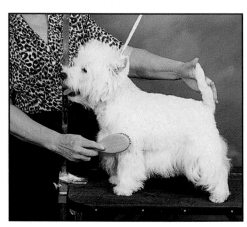

Many people who decide to own a West Highland White Terrier got their first exposure to the breed from a photo of a high-quality, beautifully groomed specimen in a book. Others may have seen Westies at a show and were captivated by their irresistible combination of looks and personality.

If you are considering owning a Westie based on pictures you've seen or dogs you've observed, you should remember that Westies don't just grow that way. Proper care involves regular grooming, and regular grooming involves a certain level of commitment. A well-groomed Westie is one of the most delightful-looking of all dogs. A neglected Westie is one of the sorriest sights you could ever see.

Grooming in Show or Pet Style

A Westie normally caries two coats—a thick, soft under-coat closer to the skin and a harsh, longer coat that is what we see. In the Scottish Highlands, the undercoat kept the dog warm and dry while the outercoat pro-tected him from thorns, brambles, dirt and sometimes even the teeth of other animals. The climate where you live may be very different from that of the Westie's native home, but the coat is still the same. The under-coat remains fairly constant at all times, but the overcoat grows until the hairs reach a certain length. At that point, the coat is blown (falls out) or dies and must be removed to make room for a fresh, new "jacket."

In the show ring, the coat is a very important factor in competition, and its natural texture must be preserved if the dog is to compete successfully. In order to main-tain that correct texture, the outer coat is either plucked or stripped out and a new coat is coaxed in. This takes about ten weeks to grow in.

Plucking means just what it says. The long outer coat is pulled out with the index finger and thumb until just the soft undercoat remains. Stripping is meant to achieve the same objective, but a stripping comb is used in place of the fingers to pull out the hairs. Purists insist that finger and thumb plucking is the only way, while others adamantly champion the use of stripping combs. Actually, best results are achieved when a com-bination of stripping and plucking is used.

Stripping and plucking are required only if a dog is to be shown. These methods are time-consuming and require considerable practice. If you hire an experi-enced groomer to strip or pluck your Westie, you will pay much more for the service than if you had the dog pet-clipped. Show-grooming is very labor-intensive whether you hire a groomer or try it yourself.

The advantages of a plucked or stripped coat are that your Westie's coat will maintain its correct harsh texture and will stay cleaner and probably shed less.

The only substantial drawback to a clipped coat is that the dog will develop a soft coat from repeated cutting. All harsh-coated terriers lose coat texture when clipped. Plucking and stripping remove the entire hair, but clipping cuts off the entire coat at the same length and makes it even with the undercoat. As a result, the coat feels softer. This may be a disadvantage for a working terrier, but is really no problem for a house pet. The clipped coat tends to retain dirt more tenaciously that the natural version, and there may be a little more shedding.

Do-It-Yourself Grooming, Yes or No?

You'll perform routine grooming at home, but you need to decide in advance who will provide the more intensive grooming your dog must have.

If you are good with your hands, you might enjoy trying your hand at trimming. You will enjoy a

If done properly, grooming sessions can be relaxing for you and your dog.

greater closeness with your Westie and save money at the same time. If you would rather leave the trimming to someone else, find a qualified groomer nearby and stay with him or her as long as you are happy with the results.

When selecting a groomer, be sure the person knows specifically how to groom a Westie. Many a Westie pet owner has gone to the grooming shop to collect their pride and joy, only to be greeted by a pet who now resembles a caricature of a Scottie or a Schnauzer. The professional who grooms your dog need not be versed in the details of hand stripping, but should know how to make a Westie look the part.

Routine Grooming

Routine grooming should be done at home. It's easy, it's relaxing, and it promotes the health and cleanliness of your Westie and the closeness your relationship. The more a Westie is groomed, the better he will look, and the healthier his skin and coat will be.

Ideally, daily grooming is wonderful, but not really necessary. If you can thoroughly groom your pet two or three times a week, he will get on just fine and you will be rewarded by the pride you take in him.

Grooming for a Westie consists, mainly, of brushing and combing. The rest involves trimming, nail and foot care, and cleaning of ears and teeth. Bathe your Westie only when and if it is necessary. Often, Westies can be made to look sparkling without ever getting near the bathtub. Keep reading and I'll tell you how.

GROOMING SUPPLIES

There are several tools you will need to make the most of your Westie's appearance. As you develop confidence and proficiency, you may add your own touches to your tool kit and your grooming skills. For starters, though, you'll need the following:

- A good-quality chrome-plated steel comb
- A soft-bristle slicker brush
- A pin brush or wig brush
- A pair of small barber's shears
- A pair of single serrated thinning shears
- A nail clipper for dogs
- Cotton
- Corn starch or powdered chalk or talc
- No-rinse dog shampoo

GROOMING THE WESTIE PUPPY

If your Westie is a young puppy when you acquire him, the grooming routine will be a little different than the grooming for an adult dog. The most important thing during grooming sessions with your puppy is that he learn how to behave and stand quietly. Many breeders will have acclimated a puppy to grooming before he goes to a new home. If the breeder of your puppy did so, you have a leg up on lifetime care. Otherwise you will have to teach your puppy, by patience and firmness, that he must not resist your efforts.

Always groom your puppy on a sturdy table with a non-skid surface. He will be safer if you do and offer less resistance to what is basically an unfamiliar ritual. Professional groomers and dog show exhibitors often use a restraining device that resembles an inverted "L" called a grooming post or grooming arm. It has a collar attached that steadies the dog being groomed. This attaches to the table and makes grooming operations generally easier. It is available from any pet supply catalog. I use one whenever I groom a dog at the shows, but at home I groom in my basement and have a lead suspended from an overhead hook. If you can do this, it works just as well.

Start grooming your Westie while he's still a puppy to familiarize him with grooming procedures.

In any case, never walk away from a dog on the grooming table. He may jump off and injure himself seriously. In a restraint, he may try to jump and accidentally hang himself if you are not close by.

When you start the grooming, talk kindly to your puppy, pick up your soft slicker brush and go over the entire body coat, brushing from head to tail. On the legs and head, brush against the lie of the coat. Now, with the metal comb, gently comb down the leg furnishings and, if there is enough hair, fluff up the hair on the head. If not, go through the motions to acclimate the puppy to what is to come.

Always keep these sessions brief, lengthening them as the puppy grows and develops more patience and confidence. The main purpose is to teach the youngster to accept grooming and keep him clean. Never do anything to a young puppy on the table that will make him resent or fear grooming sessions.

When you are done, take him off the table and tell him how handsome he is and how pleased you are with him. You might even want to reward him with a small treat. In this way, your Westie will always be a pleasure to groom and a source of pride to his entire family.

After you've brushed your Westie all over, spruce him up with a light combing.

GROOMING THE ADULT WESTIE

After your Westie has matured to the point at which he has enough hair for you to really get working on, start by misting the entire coat with water. You don't need to drench him; the point is to be able to brush him thoroughly without breaking the hairs or damaging the coat. After misting him, do a quick once-over with a natural bristle brush to help get the water through the coat.

Follow this with another once-over, this time with a pin brush. The pin brush is used mostly on the head, legs and skirt (hair under the tummy), but it does a nice job with the body coat, too. After using the pin brush,

Living with a
West Highland
White Terrier

use your slicker over the entire dog—grooming with the lie of the coat on the body and the skirt, and against the grain on the head and legs.

Follow this up with a light combing mainly to smooth down the leg furnishing and skirt and make them blend in with the body coat. Do this two or three times a week (more often, if you like) and your Westie will never develop unsightly, uncomfortable mats, and you will also be on top of any skin problems or unwelcome invasions by external parasites.

Trimming Your Westie

While it is not the purpose of this book to instruct you on the fine points of trimming a Westie, there are a few things you can do to make your pet presentable between visits to the groomer, even if that groomer is you!

After you have your Westie all brushed and combed out, start just behind the shoulders by picking up just a few hairs and gently pulling out the longest ones. Continue working a small area at a time until you have got the whole body coat reasonably even. Pull only in the direction of the growth of the coat.

TRIMMING THE EARS

Most people trim the ears with scissors. The hair on the ears should be short, and there is no fringe on the outer edges.

I stumbled on a little trick some years ago, and it has helped me tremendously in trimming Westies' ears. There was a time when I could never get the trimming on both ears to match. I'd stand in front of the dog and scissor each ear as carefully as I could, but it always looked as though the right ear pointed up and the left ear pointed out. I happen to be left-handed and was terribly frustrated by this ear-trimming problem. Truthfully, I don't remember how I arrived at my great discovery, but one day I trimmed the right ear while standing in *front* of the dog and the left ear while standing *behind* the dog. Voilà! Perfectly matched ears.

TRIMMING THE FEET

Use scissors to trim each foot to roundness. Carefully scissor any hair growing between the pads, and check for any tiny mats, stones or seeds. Remove any such debris, taking care not to nick the tender skin between the pads.

Again, learning how to trim a Westie is no small undertaking. Ask an experienced Westie breeder for help, study pictures and live dogs, or opt for the easier way out and take your Westie to a professional groomer.

Grooming for Good Health
EYES

Generally speaking, there is little the owner needs to do to care for a Westie's eyes. It is normal for a small amount of matter to collect at the inner corner of the eyes. Check this every ten days or so, and gently remove any accumulation with a moistened cotton ball. If there appears to be considerable amounts of matter, or if the matter is wet and mucousy, you might want to call it to the attention of your veterinarian. If there is a problem, he or she can prescribe an appropriate medication and regimen.

EARS

We are routinely advised that erect-eared dogs are less prone to ear infections than dogs in whom the ear canal is all or partially covered. Certainly, this is true, but that doesn't mean that your erect-eared Westie doesn't require ear care.

During a thorough grooming session, check your Westie's ears. If necessary, gently pluck out any long hair that you can grasp growing from the ear canal. Wipe out the canal with a cotton ball moistened with a little alcohol. If you keep to this regimen, your Westie should never be troubled with ear infections. If you notice your Westie shaking his head or pawing at his ears, or if you notice a dark discharge at the ear opening or an unpleasant odor, a trip to the veterinarian is in order.

While you're grooming, check your Westie's ears for any unusual discharge.

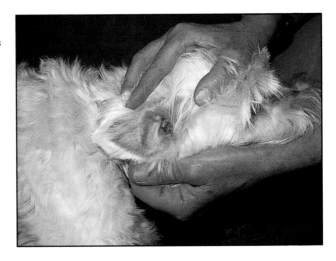

NAILS

Ideally, a Westie's nails should be black, but many are not. If your Westie has light-colored nails, you are lucky when it comes to pedicure. There is a vein running through each nail on a dog's foot that carries a blood supply. This is called the quick, and it will bleed profusely if cut. It is much easier to err on a dog with black nails than on one with clear ones.

It is easy to cut your dog's nails. You simply have to make him behave during grooming sessions. The most popular kind of nail cutter is called the guillotine because of the way it cuts. It is an efficient, easy-to-use implement and can be found wherever pet supplies are sold.

I like to hold the aperture at an angle from the bottom of the nail to the top. After making the first cut, I trim the points off the sides; this exposes the quick without causing any bleeding, and the dog's normal activity helps shorten the nails further.

If your Westie still has his dewclaws (fifth toe on front foot), you will need to keep an eye on them to prevent them from growing too long. Left unattended, dewclaws can grow around in a circle and actually pierce the dog's skin. With dewclaws, simply clip the portion beyond the quick as required.

TEETH AND GUMS

If your Westie is still a young puppy when he joins your household, you will have to see him through all or part of the teething stage. Furnish the puppy with safe, "approved" chewing articles until this stage of puppyhood is passed.

As an extra precaution, you might want to use bitter apple or Tabasco sauce on anything you wish to protect from busy jaws. Terriers grow big teeth, so take care to protect your things while permanent dentition is developing.

Healthy teeth will be strong, sound and clean, and healthy gums will be firm and pink. There is no reason for a well-groomed dog to suffer from the effects of neglected oral hygiene.

While your puppy is still quite young, accustom him to having his mouth opened and his teeth and gums gently touched during grooming sessions. It is probably better not to follow this up while the puppy teeth are coming in, but the object is to teach him to remain still during any kind of oral grooming. Use a small gauze pad wrapped around your finger to rub the teeth. This will help remove soft plaque and help him accept having his teeth handled.

Eventually you may want to use a dentifrice and a toothbrush especially made for dogs. Weekly attention to his mouth will help him keep his teeth and remain healthy well into old age. If you do this regularly, your Westie will never need to be anesthetized to have his teeth cleaned. He will never be bothered with the pain of periodontal disease, and, for the most part, his breath will never clear out a room!

GROOMING TOOLS

pin brush
slicker brush
flea comb
towel
mat rake
grooming glove
scissors
nail clippers
tooth-cleaning equipment
shampoo
conditioner
clippers

6
Grooming Your West Highland White Terrier

Keeping Your Westie White

I never cease to be amazed at the number of city-dwellers who seek out Westies as pets in spite of the difficulty of keeping a small, white dog clean in a typical urban setting. But they do, and many learn to tackle cleaning with capable good humor.

BATHING YOUR WESTIE

For most pet owners, keeping a dog clean means bathing, but bathing your Westie too often is not a great idea. When a bath is in order, however, there is a right way to do it. Here's how. If you can bathe your Westie in a raised sink, you and he will be much better off than if you try it bending over a bathtub. After a thorough brushing, put the dog in the sink and insert cotton in his ears to keep the water out.

Wash your Westie in the sink, using a shampoo formulated especially for white dogs.

Now you are ready to bathe him, but don't fill the sink at all. Most kitchen sinks have a spray hose, or you can buy one. Adjust the water to be a little hotter than lukewarm, and wet the dog's body thoroughly with the hose, saving the head for last. After the coat is thoroughly wet, pour a small amount of shampoo made for white dogs down the spine and, using a sponge, lather thoroughly, working with the lie of the coat. Make sure you soap the skirt and the legs. Save the head for last, taking care to keep water out of the ears and the eyes.

Now rinse out all the shampoo. If the dog still looks a bit dingy, repeat the process. After you have rinsed all the shampoo out of the coat, squeeze as much excess moisture from the skirt and legs as you can, wrap the dog in a large towel and blot the towel over him to keep from getting soaked yourself.

Drying Your Westie

After toweling, use a hand-held hair dryer set on warm-high and brush him with the pin brush while the coat is drying. Go with the lie of the coat, except for head and legs, and keep at it until the dog is thoroughly dry. Many Westie owners advise just washing the head, skirt and legs and cleaning the body by other means.

Alternatives to Bathing

Several companies manufacture waterless shampoos for dogs that obviate the need for bathing. These are applied to the coat, rubbed in, toweled and dried in the usual manner. They are very convenient and work nicely, but are not very effective if a dog is really soiled. Then, only a sink bath will do the trick.

Let's suppose you have taken your Westie for a walk in the park and he has come home rather grimy on his legs and undercarriage. What do you do? First, put him in his crate and let him dry naturally. Then put him on the grooming table and rub powdered chalk, talc or cornstarch into his coat. Allow it to dry, then brush it out and you will be amazed to find that your Westie is sparklingly pristine again.

Healthy Skin

Today's prospective pet owner is usually more aware of breed-specific health problems than his counterpart of the past. While the matter of a Westie's health will be taken up in more detail in chapter 7, it is appropriate to discuss skin health here as it relates to grooming in the West Highland White Terrier.

Skin diseases are, unfortunately, frequently associated with the breed. These can take many forms and present a varying degree of severity.

If you notice a skin problem, take the puppy to your vet to determine the exact nature of the condition. At the same time, get the vet's recommendations on treatment, including the right medicated shampoo and the right way to use it. With a little time and patience, many skin conditions can be effectively controlled.

Closing Thoughts on Grooming a Westie

You are probably reading this book because you are considering getting a pet you want to be proud of, or because you already have a Westie and are proud of him. Think how your pride will be enhanced when you know your saucy, white-coated friend is aware of his good looks and overall well-being. A few short sessions every week to groom your Westie will make him look his best. Then, as you stroll through the park or the mall together, you can enjoy the admiring glances your handsome, well-cared-for Westie is bound to attract. It's a lovely experience; promise yourself you'll try it soon.

chapter 7

Keeping Your
West Highland
White Terrier
Healthy

Today, the owner of a West Highland White Terrier is truly fortunate, and for many reasons. Given a reasonable level of consistent, attentive care, most Westies will enjoy at least a dozen happy years. My wife's first Westie lived for almost eighteen years, and that little dog had a really rocky start in life.

Another reason for the good fortune of today's Westie owner

is one shared by all dog owners. Modern advances in veterinary science have done for our dogs what advances in human medicine have done for us. Today, your Westie can look forward to a lifetime of better health care in both routine and unusual situations.

Preventive Care

The easiest way to make sure your Westie remains healthy and sound is to make preventive care a priority from the start. This will require a minimal amount of effort on your part, and will mean less money in vet bills and less heartache and discomfort for you and your Westie later on.

The grooming procedures discussed in Chapter 6 should be followed routinely, including ear and teeth cleaning and other health-maintenance procedures. While you are grooming your Westie, feel for lumps and any other irregularities that might indicate a problem. Early detection can make a great difference in many conditions.

Choose a knowledgeable veterinarian, and establish a good working relationship with him or her. Follow the vaccination schedule you devise with your vet and be sure to follow up with boosters when necessary.

Keeping your puppy's environment safe and clean will do much to minimize potential hazards. Keep your puppy on a leash or in an enclosed yard, and make sure she has some basic obedience training. This will help to make sure your pup heeds your commands when necessary. If you are trying to call her near a busy street, you need to be reasonably sure she won't tear off into oncoming traffic.

> ## YOUR PUPPY'S VACCINES
>
> Vaccines are given to prevent your dog from getting an infectious disease like canine distemper or rabies. Vaccines are the ultimate preventive medicine: they're given before your dog ever gets the disease so as to protect him from the disease. That's why it is necessary for your dog to be vaccinated routinely. Puppy vaccines start at eight weeks of age for the five-in-one DHLPP vaccine and are given every three to four weeks until the puppy is sixteen months old. Your veterinarian will put your puppy on a proper schedule and will remind you when to bring in your dog for shots.

Finding the Right Veterinarian

Locating the right veterinarian is a matter of the highest priority for you and your Westie. While there is likely to be at least one veterinarian practicing close to your home, that doesn't mean that he or she is the best qualified care provider. Get a veterinary referral from a Westie breeder in your area, or ask other dog owners in your area about their veterinarians. Armed with this information, you can then sally forth to develop your own impressions and find the veterinarian you like and can work with.

Just as location is not the most important consideration in choosing the most suitable vet, neither is price. Today, the cost of veterinary attention for your dog is not cheap by any standard, so it is important to know that you will always get what you pay for. Never bargain shop for your dog's health needs.

Puppies are particularly vulnerable to diseases, so make sure you stick to the vaccination schedule you've set up with your veterinarian.

Try to visit all the practices you are interested in before actually getting your Westie. Check for a cheerful, clean waiting room and a welcoming, helpful receptionist. Determine what the office hours are and what arrangements are in place for emergencies. Some veterinarians will make house calls, and in some locations the veterinarians take turns keeping their clinics open after normal hours to meet the needs of their community. In some cities, large, fully equipped hospitals are available around the clock to meet any need of any pet owner.

Try to find out whether the veterinarian you are considering is experienced with Westies. This is very important in dealing with any breed-specific problems your dog may develop. If you can meet the veterinarian before an office visit, even for a few minutes, it can help you feel more at ease with the doctor when your relationship becomes a functioning one.

Vaccinations

A puppy's first immunity is acquired from her mother in a substance called *colostrum,* which is in the mother's milk during the first twenty-four or thirty-six hours after the puppy is born. This immunity lasts for the first few months of a puppy's life. As this natural immunity wears off, artificial immunity, in the form of vaccinations, must be substituted.

One of the most important items on your agenda on the day you get your new Westie puppy is to get a copy of her health records. This will include the types and names of all inoculations, and when they were given, as well as a complete list of wormings. Take this to your veterinarian on your first visit, and she or he will set up a schedule to continue these inoculations.

Keep to the vaccination schedule religiously, and don't let your puppy outdoors until your veterinarian says you can. It will take a few days for the shot to provide complete protection.

The diseases your puppy needs to be vaccinated against include distemper, hepatitis, parainfluenza and leptospirosis. All the diseases your puppy needs protection from have specific symptoms and means of transmission.

Distemper is a viral disease and is highly contagious. An affected dog will run a high fever, cough, vomit, have diarrhea and seizures. These symptoms will worsen, ultimately leading to death.

WHEN TO CALL THE VET

In any emergency situation, you should call your veterinarian immediately. You can make the difference in your dog's life by staying as calm as possible when you call and by giving the doctor or the assistant as much information as possible before you leave for the clinic. That way, the vet will be able to take immediate, specific action to remedy your dog's situation.

Emergencies include acute abdominal pain, suspected poisoning, snakebite, burns, frostbite, shock, dehydration, abnormal vomiting or bleeding, and deep wounds. You are the best judge of your dog's health, as you live with and observe him every day. Don't hesitate to call your veterinarian if you suspect trouble.

Hepatitis is a liver disorder characterized by fever, abdominal pain, vomiting and diarrhea.

Parainfluenza, also known as "kennel cough," is a very contagious upper respiratory infection characterized by a dry, nonproductive cough. The mode of inoculation for parainfluenza is usually through the nostrils, with a specially adapted syringe tip. Because there are so many strains of this disease (much like the flu in humans), one vaccine cannot prevent them all. However, if you are planning on making any kind of trip to another location or will be boarding your puppy in a kennel facility, a parainfluenza shot is heartily advised.

Leptospirosis is a bacterial disease spread by the urine of infected animals. Mice and rats are especially implicated in transmission, so protection is a good idea. However, it's a good idea to speak to the vet about this vaccination beforehand, because the leptospirosis shot sometimes results in a bad reaction in the puppy.

More recently the viral diseases *parvovirus* and *coronavirus* have become noteworthy health problems among companion dogs. Affected dogs show a high fever and bloody and/or mucoid diarrhea. Their behavior is lethargic, and they are in great peril as these dangerous diseases are often fatal. Happily, there is protection against both these killers. Get your puppy inoculated, and keep her away from sickly-looking dogs or places where many dogs congregate.

Dogs owners are required by law to have their pets inoculated for **rabies.** This disease is characterized by altered behavior; shy animals may appear friendly or aggressive. As the virus spreads, the animal will begin to salivate excessively and drool. There is no cure for rabies in dogs. People who have been bitten by a rabid animal must endure a long and painful series of shots. This is one vaccine that is not optional, with good reason!

BOOSTER SHOTS

After your puppy gets her first permanent shot, she should have an annual booster. Always keep your

Westie's shots current. You open a door to disaster for your pet when you let boosters slide.

The Useful Thermometer

Did you notice how many of the diseases mentioned in the last section have high fever as a symptom? Knowing this, it is a wise idea to keep a reliable rectal thermometer handy for your dog. Learn how to use it, and insist that the puppy stand still while you are taking her temperature. If you have even the slightest suspicion that your puppy is off-color, the first thing to do is take her temperature. It's very easy to do and will help your veterinarian make a more accurate diagnosis.

A dog's normal temperature is about 101.5 degrees Fahrenheit, and it is always taken rectally. To take a dog's temperature, first place her on a table or other raised, skid-proof surface and assure her that all is well. With a conventional thermometer, lubricate the tip and gently insert the thermometer into the anus to about one-third of the thermometer's length. Hold the dog in position, with the thermometer in place for two or three minutes. At the end of that time, remove the thermometer, wipe it gently and take the reading. Obviously, you should also wipe the thermometer with an alcohol-soaked tissue before and after each use.

If you use a digital thermometer, simply follow the manufacturer's directions.

Internal Parasites

There's no getting away from it—worms are a fact of life, but you can do a lot to make sure they don't cause problems for your Westie.

When you pick up your puppy, you should be given, along with the vaccination schedule, the dates of the puppy's previous wormings and the names of the drugs that were used. When you take your new puppy to the veterinarian for that first checkup, take her medical history, and take along a stool sample as well. The veterinarian will examine it and determine what kind of worms, if any, are present. She or he will also give you the appropriate medicine and instruct you on the dosage.

In most cases, worming a puppy is a pretty straight forward matter, and today's medications are much easier on a puppy's delicate system than were the remedies of years ago. Don't ignore a worm infestation, but know that such conditions are not unusual and will respond to proper treatment.

ROUNDWORMS

These worms are extremely common and can infest even unborn puppies, passing through the placenta to establish themselves. In heavy infestations, it is not unusual to see live roundworms in a puppy stool. Roundworms can even be vomited up. They get their name by their tendency to curl up when exposed to air.

Symptoms of roundworm infestation include a pot belly and a dull coat. Diarrhea and vomiting are other clues to the presence of these worms. Your veterinarian can dispense the right drugs to expel the pests, and you will probably need to repeat the dosage about ten days later to break the worm's life cycle and get rid of worms that matured after your initial dosing. For puppies, roundworms can be especially serious, so if your puppy has them, act fast.

Common internal parasites (l-r): roundworm, whipworm, tapeworm and hookworm.

TAPEWORM

Tapeworm is another common external parasite and is usually spread by fleas, which act as intermediate hosts. A dog troubled with a flea infestation may swallow some fleas while biting at itchy flea bites, and in the process ingest tapeworm eggs. Tapeworms are long, segmented parasites, and the fresh, moving segments are often plainly visible in a stool. Dried segments stuck to the dog's hair near the anus resemble grains of brown rice. A tapeworm-affected dog may have diarrhea, dry skin or appear underweight. She may bite at her hind-quarters or "scoot" them along the ground. Again, follow the veterinarian's directions and remember to treat your dog and household surroundings for fleas.

HOOKWORM

Hookworm is a common cause of anemia and is particularly devastating to young puppies. The parasite gets a good foothold when hygienic conditions are not observed or when dogs are exposed to contaminated areas. A dog may swallow larvae, or the worm may penetrate the dog's skin. Eggs are identifiable through microscopic examination from a fresh stool sample. Your veterinarian can dispense drugs to combat hookworm, but it is also necessary to keep your surroundings clean and prevent the puppy from contact with feces and other animals.

WHIPWORM

Suspect whipworm if your dog is passing a watery or mucoid stool, shows weakness, weight loss, general symptoms of anemia or appears to be in overall poor condition. Whipworm is not visible to the naked eye, so determination of infestation is up to your veterinarian and his or her microscope. If your dog does have whipworm, you will probably have to have several stool checks done and institute a regimen of medication prescribed by your veterinarian.

Treating your dog for whipworm, by itself, is not enough. Whipworms, like so many other internal parasites, thrive in and are contracted from contaminated soil and unsanitary conditions. Sanitation and strict monitoring are important to keeping your dog clear of whipworm and all the other insidious parasites that can infest your dog.

HEARTWORM

Heartworm was once considered a problem confined largely to the southern United States. Unfortunately, this parasite has proliferated and is a cause for concern in most areas. The condition is passed by the bite of a mosquito infected with the heartworm larvae. It may take some time for the symptoms to show, and by that time, heroic measures may be needed to restore a dog's health.

It is far easier and wiser to use preventive measures to protect your Westie from heartworm infestation. Your veterinarian will draw a blood sample from your dog at the appropriate time and examine it under a microscope for heartworm microfillaria. In the probable event that your dog is negative for heartworm, your veterinarian will dispense the pills or syrup your dog needs to remain free of the parasite.

Dosage depends on the dog's weight and is administered either daily or monthly. Some owners suspend medication after the first killing frost and resume when the weather get warm. Those who live in places where the weather is always warm enough to support the mosquito's life cycle must keep the medication going the year round. We keep our Westies on the monthly preventive regimen all year. Suspect heartworm if your dog exhibits a chronic cough and a general weakness, with an unexplained loss of weight. If your dog tests positive, your veterinarian is the only person qualified to treat her.

PROTOZOANS

Not all internal parasites are worms. Tiny, single-celled organisms called protozoans can also wreak havoc in your Westie's internal mechanisms, but effective treatment is available. The most common disorders in dogs caused by protozoans are coccidiosis and giardiasis.

Coccidiosis is generally the result of poor hygienic conditions in the dog's surroundings. The symptoms of this inflammation of the intestinal tract include sometimes bloody diarrhea, a generally poor appearance, cough, runny eyes, and nasal and eye discharges. The disease is more serious in puppies, who are less resistant.

Giardiasis comes from drinking water contaminated with the disease-causing organism. As with coccidiosis, diarrhea is the symptom to watch for. A veterinarian must make the definite diagnosis.

External Parasites
FLEAS

For your Westie, a good scratch is one of life's little pleasures. However, if your Westie appears to be spend-

The flea is a die-hard pest.

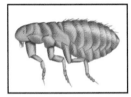

ing a lot of time scratching herself and doing so with a vengeance, you should take a closer look. If your Westie's skin looks red and irritated and there are little dark flecks throughout her coat, fleas may have set up house-keeping with your pet as their primary host. Bad news? Absolutely, but there are things you can do about it.

If your Westie seems to be scratching a lot, take a closer look to determine if she has fleas.

With a flea infestation, you must be tenacious about getting rid of these nuisances. If you do nothing, the fleas will do plenty.

First, treat your dog. She should be dipped and given a good bath with a flea and tick shampoo. Be cautious here as some preparations will turn a Westie's coat pink.

Getting the fleas off your Westie alone is not enough. You must also treat your home and yard. Destroy any contaminated bedding, and go over the dog's entire environment with a spray or fogger to kill all the fleas. This means outdoors as well as inside the home. And even with all this, you must exercise common sense in other matters regarding flea control.

Many Westies have violent reactions to flea bites. As you will see a bit further on, skin health is an issue in this breed and flea allergy dermatitis is looked upon as a serious problem. Even if you do get rid of the fleas, keep a close watch on your pet. Any return of those dark flecks (dried, excreted blood the flea has taken from your dog), irritated skin, rough-looking coat or excessive scratching should start you looking again.

> ### FIGHTING FLEAS
>
> Remember, the fleas you see on your dog are only part of the problem—the smallest part! To rid your dog and home of fleas, you need to treat your dog *and* your home. Here's how:
>
> • Identify where your pet(s) sleep. These are "hot spots."
>
> • Clean your pets' bedding regularly by vacuuming and washing.
>
> • Spray "hot spots" with a non-toxic, long-lasting flea larvicide.
>
> • Treat outdoor "hot spots" with insecticide.
>
> • Kill eggs on pets with a product containing insect growth regulators (IGRs).
>
> • Kill fleas on pets per your veterinarian's recommendation.

TICKS

Ticks look like tiny spiders. They attach themselves to a passing dog, suck blood from the dog, mate, and drop off, and the females lay thousands of eggs to begin the life cycle yet again. In the course of feeding, the female, which is much larger than the male, becomes engorged with blood and about the size of a pea.

Three types of ticks (l-r): the wood tick, brown dog tick and deer tick.

As with fleas, you must rid your dog and your environment of ticks if your control is to be effective.

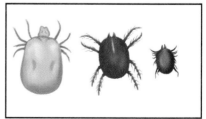

Ticks are not as active as fleas, so removing them is a little easier. Go over the entire dog with a pair of tweezers; do not attempt to remove ticks with your fingers. Westie owners unlucky enough to have to deal with ticks can take comfort from the fact that the

Living with a
West Highland
White Terrier

white coat makes it easier to find the little vampires. When you find a tick, drip a little alcohol directly on it. The alcohol will asphyxiate the tick, causing it to release its hold. Pull it off with tweezers, and drop the tick into a small cup of alcohol, where it will drown and trouble your dog no more. Diligence is the watchword with tick control. Once you've gotten rid of the ticks, keep your dog out of those wild, woodsy places where ticks hide, waiting for your unsuspecting Westie to come along and be their meal ticket.

Use tweezers to remove ticks from your dog.

Also remember that there are several kinds of ticks, and you should know which species are common to your area. The brown dog tick is probably the most common species, but there is a species that can spread Rocky Mountain Spotted Fever, and the deer tick is the mode of transmission for Lyme disease. Lyme disease, like Spotted Fever, can be passed to humans, so be very careful if you find that your dog has a tick infestation. If your dog appears lame for no known reason, she may have contracted Lyme disease and will require veterinary attention.

In checking your Westie for ticks, pay particular attention to the face, the base of the ears, between the toes and the skin around the anus—all places ticks seem to congregate.

LICE

Happily, these annoyingly persistent creatures are infrequently encountered in this age of enlightened hygiene. However, any dog can contract lice from any infested animal. Lice cause pronounced itching and are an annoying problem neither your dog nor you need. If your dog is harboring lice, treatment is the same as for fleas—a good bath and a dip that does the job.

Mites infest different areas of a dog's body. You might say the various species are specialists of a sort.

The **ear mite** (*Otodectes cynotis*) is a common problem for dogs with dropped ears, but even Westies with their erect ears can be troubled by them. If your Westie seems constantly to be scratching at her ears and if, on examination, you notice a dark, crumbly, malodorous accumulation, your dog has ear mites and must be treated for them. Your veterinarian can give you medication and instructions for clearing up the problem.

Scabies, or sarcoptic mange, is yet another condition related to mite infestation. The causative agent, *Sarcoptes scabei*, is a microscopic organism that burrows under the host's skin, causing intense itching and hair loss. This condition can also be passed to humans. Left untreated, it can spread to a dog's entire body.

Demodetic mange is the name of the condition spread by *Demodex canis*. The mite lives in the dog's hair follicles, causing hair loss and red, thickened skin. Eventually pustules form in infected follicles. Diagnosis via skin scrapings is required, and medicated dips are the treatment of choice to destroy these mites.

Spaying and Neutering

There are many reasons you should consider spaying or neutering your pet Westie—more than you probably think. If you own a pet Westie or are currently trying to locate one, you are probably interested only in the companionship aspect of the breed. And that's just what you should be interested in. Your female Westie does not have to have a canine family to be fulfilled; she has a human one. You are the center of her universe, and she doesn't need anything or anyone else. If you have your Westie female spayed at the proper time, she will never get the urge to mate and she won't miss it.

In addition, you will not have to suffer the hassle of heat cycles. While your female is in heat, you must keep a *very* careful watch on her all the time, and make sure no males have access to her. Suitors can become quite aggressive in their pursuits and may mark your home to show their territory. In addition, you will have to make sure your female wears a "diaper" so she does not soil your home or car. You will have to make sure it does not slip or leak.

ADVANTAGES OF SPAY/NEUTER

The greatest advantage of spaying (for females) or neutering (for males) your dog is that you are guaranteed your dog will not produce puppies. There are too many puppies already available for too few homes. There are other advantages as well.

ADVANTAGES OF SPAYING

No messy heats.

No "suitors" howling at your windows or waiting in your yard.

Decreased incidences of pyometra (disease of the uterus) and breast cancer.

ADVANTAGES OF NEUTERING

Lessens male aggressive and territorial behaviors, but doesn't affect the dog's personality. Behaviors are often owner-induced, so neutering is not the only answer, but it is a good start.

Prevents the need to roam in search of bitches in season.

Decreased incidences of urogenital diseases.

If you have your male Westie neutered, he will be better able to focus on being the family pet than the frustrated lothario. He will not have the urge to roam in search of potential mates and will probably be cleaner at home.

There are numerous health benefits that make spaying or neutering your Westie the wisest choice. Spayed females are at no risk for pyometra, a life-threatening uterine infection that often affects older, intact females. Spaying and neutering has been determined to reduce the incidence of cancer in older dogs by as much as 90 percent. These reasons alone should persuade you that spaying or neutering your Westie is the kindest thing you can do for your pet.

You may think that, after all, you paid a fairly high price for your new pride and joy and that having a litter may seem a nice way to turn a good dollar. Believe me, it isn't.

Breeding dogs as they should be bred involves endless hours of hard work and significant expenses for veterinary services, foods, vitamin supplements and much more. There are usually stud fees to pay, and sometimes long-distance shipping is involved to abet Cupid's course. Not every mating is successful, and not every successful mating results in the number, sex and quality of puppies the breeder was hoping for. Any Westie breeder can tell you horror stories of losing whole litters of puppies when all should have been well.

There is one more reason why pet owners should not breed their Westies. The shocking volume of unwanted, homeless dogs euthanized in America every year is a national disgrace. Why would any right-thinking dog lover want to add to that grisly statistic? I always tell this to people who call or visit and ask about breeding. One should breed only if one is a serious prospective fancier or an established one, and then only to better the breed.

Often, when one buys a Westie puppy, it will be on the condition that the buyer signs a spay/neuter agreement. I can't urge strongly enough that you sign willingly. You and your Westie will be better for it.

As far as when to have the spay or neuter operation, let your veterinarian be your guide. Some doctors prefer early neutering; others are willing to wait. In my opinion, a bitch should have gone through her first season before she is spayed. That way she will have desirable feminine characteristics before the surgery and keep them for the rest of her life. As most Westie bitches come in season for the first time at about eight months, that gives your puppy plenty of time to get comfortable with you and her new home before the surgery is done. Male puppies should be neutered at about the same age.

To give a pill, open the mouth wide, then drop it in the back of the throat.

Administering Medications

Whenever you must give medication to your Westie, you must always remember that you are dealing with a very clever individual. Westies are experts at spitting pills right back at you, or hiding them under the tongue in the cheek and spitting them out when you aren't looking. So make sure the medication is swallowed before releasing the dog.

TO GIVE A PILL

Pills are easier to give once you have mastered the moves. To give a pill, place the dog in front of you a little lower than eye level on a raised surface. Gently open the dog's mouth and place the pill at the back of the tongue and use your thumb to push it toward the esophagus. Hold your Westie's jaws shut with the muzzle pointing up until you see her swallow. This is your signal that the pill was taken. With stubborn cases, you might have to gently press the nostrils closed until the dog swallows to get air.

TO ADMINISTER LIQUID MEDICATION

These are better administered with a special syringe. These syringes are made for human babies and are

available in any drugstore. The dosage is sure, and the dog will not end up wearing the medication as she might if you tried to use a spoon.

SNEAKY ALTERNATIVES

If the straightforward methods above don't seem to be working for you, there are other sneakier possibilities. They are 1) rolling a pill in a little ball of liverwurst or cream cheese or 2) putting the pill or liquid in her dinner. The first sneaky alternative always works. The second works only if the dog is a chowhound and doesn't stop to check what's in her bowl. Some Westies do, so be forewarned and take whatever measures become necessary to medicate your Westie as needed.

Squeeze eye ointment into the lower lid.

ADMINISTERING EYE MEDICATION

Hold the dog firmly. Pull out the lower eyelid to form a little pocket. Squeeze the directed amount of ointment into the pocket. When the dog blinks, the medication will be distributed over the eye. Offer lots of praise afterwards.

ELIZABETHAN COLLAR

Often, as treatment for skin irritation and other conditions, the vet will prescribe topical ointment. The application is simple: just part the hair and gently rub the ointment on the affected area. Because your Westie's first reaction to the medication will probably

An Elizabethan collar keeps your dog from licking a fresh wound.

be to lick it off, your vet might also give you an Elizabethan collar for your Westie to wear. This cone-shaped collar prevents your dog from chewing or licking, and thus further irritating, the troubled spot. Your Westie will want you to think she is quite miserable in this gadget, but she must keep it on to help the wound heal more quickly and to keep it from becoming infected. Do your best to see she wears it as long as the vet recommends.

First Aid and Emergency Care

Life for our dogs, as for us, always involves uncertainty. That is why you need to have some ability to minister to your dog in the event of a sudden illness or injury.

Use a scarf or old hose to make a temporary muzzle, as shown.

MUZZLING

The first thing you should know how to do is to handle and transport an injured animal safely. A dog in pain is probably not going to recognize her owner or realize that people are trying to help her. In those circumstances, she is likely to bite. The dog in trouble needs to be muzzled, and the diagrams in this chapter show how an emergency muzzle made of gauze or a necktie can be fashioned and applied.

TRANSPORTING YOUR DOG IN AN EMERGENCY

An emergency stretcher can be made from a blanket and, depending on the size of the dog, carried by two or more people. An injured dog can also be carried on a rigid board, in a box or wrapped in a towel and carried in a person's arms. Care should be taken, though, that the manner of transport does not exacerbate the dog's original injury.

SHOCK

If a dog is in shock, keep her as warm and as quiet as possible and get her emergency veterinary attention at once. You may need to control hemorrhaging until professional help can be found.

When you are faced with a dog in shock, either from a severe trauma or a profound disease symptom, you may need to administer either artificial respiration or CPR.

ARTIFICIAL RESPIRATION

Apply artificial respiration when there is no perceptible breathing, but be alert to any movement from the dog as you are also exposed to a potential bite wound. Open the dog's mouth, clearing any obstructions. Depress the tongue and look into the throat to be sure it is also unobstructed. Any fluids or other material that could impede the passage of air should be removed at this time. Now gently hold the mouth closed while you inhale. Cover the dog's nose with your mouth and exhale gently; there is no need to blow hard. As you carefully force air into the dog's lung, watch the chest cavity for expansion. This rhythm should be repeated about every five or six seconds, or ten or twelve breaths per minute.

CPR

If you are trying to administer first aid to an injured dog and cannot detect a heartbeat, you will have to administer CPR (cardiopulmonary resuscitation). If you have already been trained in CPR techniques for people, you have an advantage. If not, do your best.

For dogs, lay the patient on her right side, placing both hands over the heart. With a dog as small as a Westie, one hand on either side of the chest will do. Press on the chest firmly at a rate of about seventy to one hundred times per minute, but take care not to press too hard or you might break some ribs as you attempt to reestablish the heartbeat.

BLEEDING

If your dog is bleeding, direct pressure is an effective way to staunch the flow. You can fashion a pressure dressing from gauze or some strong fabric. Wrap the area of the wound, applying even pressure as you apply the gauze strips. If you notice tissue swelling below the site of the wound, ease the pressure or, if necessary, remove the bandage altogether. If you have no gauze, use any clean cloth or your hand as a last resort. For arterial bleeding, you will proba-

Run your hands regularly over your dog to feel for any injuries.

bly need a tourniquet along with the pressure bandage. You may use gauze strips, cloth or any other material that can be wrapped tightly between the wound and the heart to slow the flow of blood. With a tourniquet, you must remember to loosen the pressure about every ten minutes. Get the injured dog to a veterinarian as soon as possible.

DIARRHEA

Diarrhea is often the normal result of your dog having eaten something she shouldn't have. However, it can also be the symptom of something more serious, and in young puppies, it can cause dehydration quickly. If diarrhea continues for more than twenty-four hours, or if you notice any other symptoms, call your vet immediately.

Make a temporary splint by wrapping the leg in firm casing, then bandaging it.

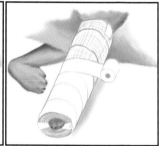

BROKEN BONES

With fractures, you must determine how to help the dog without doing more harm than good. The area of the fracture should be immobilized with the use of a splint or a rolled-up magazine secured with gauze or similar material, and the area should be cushioned to support it as much as possible. In compound fractures, the broken bone will pierce the skin; this is more serious than a simple fracture and should be covered in preparation for transfer to a veterinarian. Fractures are very painful, and the injured dog must be handled with great care and probably muzzled for the safety of all who will handle her.

HEATSTROKE

The Westie's system is admirably suited to the cold, but far less efficient in heat. Dogs can die from heatstroke easily. Every year dogs die unnecessarily by being locked in closed cars during warm weather. Regardless of the season, a dog showing signs of heat distress—rapid, shallow breathing and a rapid heartbeat—needs to be cooled down immediately. Spraying or soaking the dog with cold water, or pressing an ice bag or freezer pack against the groin, abdomen, anus, neck and forehead are all effective in bringing down the stricken dog's temperature.

It is said that a dog who has suffered an episode of heatstroke will always be more susceptible to future incidents of heat-related distress. Of course, heatstroke is easier to prevent than it is to treat. During warm weather, allow your Westie to exercise either early in the morning or in the evening, avoiding the hottest part of the day. Allow her free access to cool, fresh water and take her in the car only if you absolutely must. A Westie's white coat gives her a little more tolerance to heat and sun than dark-colored dogs, but this is not a reason to be less than vigilant.

CHOKING

If your Westie is choking, you must act quickly to find and dislodge the foreign object after securing the mouth open by inserting a rigid object between the molars on one side. Use your fingers or, very carefully, use long-nosed pliers or a hemostat to withdraw the object. The Heimlich maneuver can also be used for choking dogs; ask your veterinarian to demonstrate how it's done. If your choking dog is not breathing, you will have to resort to artificial respiration.

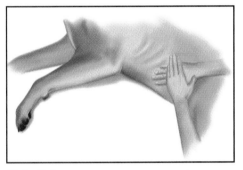

Applying abdominal thrusts can save a choking dog.

CONVULSIONS

Dogs going through convulsions should be cushioned to avoid self-injury, and you must avoid putting a hand near the mouth of a seizuring dog. Such dogs are not likely to swallow their tongues during an episode, but it is a wise idea to have the dog examined by a veterinarian to determine the cause and means of

Living with a West Highland White Terrier

control. Canine convulsions often respond to a drug-based therapy. See your veterinarian as soon as possible to evaluate the problem and begin a course of appropriate medication.

A FIRST-AID KIT

Keep a canine first-aid kit on hand for general care and emergencies. Check it periodically to make sure liquids haven't spilled or dried up, and replace medications and materials after they're used. Your kit should include:

Activated charcoal tablets

Adhesive tape
(1 and 2 inches wide)

Antibacterial ointment
(for skin and eyes)

Aspirin (buffered or enteric coated, *not* Ibuprofen)

Bandages: Gauze rolls (1 and 2 inches wide) and dressing pads

Cotton balls

Diarrhea medicine

Dosing syringe

Hydrogen peroxide (3%)

Petroleum jelly

Rectal thermometer

Rubber gloves

Rubbing alcohol

Scissors

Tourniquet

Towel

Tweezers

LAMENESS

A Westie can go lame for a wide variety of reasons. She can cut a pad, pick up a foreign body (like a thorn) or break a nail. All these things will cause lameness. For cuts, clean the area and apply an antiseptic. If the wound is deep, staunch the bleeding and get your Westie to the vet. Also, for a painful broken nail, visit your veterinarian as soon as possible. He or she will medicate the injury to promote healing. With a broken nail, the vet will trim off as much as possible and cauterize and wrap the dog's paw.

INSECT BITES

If your Westie is bitten by any stinging insect, remove the stinger, apply a baking soda paste to the affected area, and stop the swelling and pain with an ice bag or cold pack. It would be a wise idea to run your pet's wounds past your vet to be sure all is well. An antibiotic may be prescribed.

Bee stings are painful, but even more serious is the possibility that your dog is allergic to them. If so, the sting will start to swell immediately. If this happens, get your Westie to the vet as soon as possible. He or she will administer an antihistamine or other treatment.

ANIMAL BITES

If your Westie is bitten by another animal, follow the same procedures you would for another kind of bleeding wound: apply pressure until the bleeding has stopped, and cleanse thoroughly with hydrogen peroxide. Follow up with a visit to the vet if the wound looks serious; stitches may be required. If your Westie was bitten by a wild animal, inform your local animal control bureau. The animal may be rabid and any information you can provide the authorities with will be helpful.

BURNS

If your dog suffers a burn, use cold water soaks on affected areas and get veterinary help as soon as possible.

POISONING

There are numerous preparations in the home that can be dangerous to dogs. Antifreeze, insecticides, various medicines and cosmetics could all be dangerous to your dog.

In the outdoors, your dog could get into a wide variety of plants that could make her sick. Become familiar with the toxic plants in your vicinity, and make sure to keep your dog away from anything poisonous.

Some of the many household substances harmful to your dog.

If your dog has been poisoned and you know the substance, use the antidote given on the label of the container. Otherwise, call the National Animal Poison Control Center hotline at 1-800-548-2423.

VOMITING

Your dog will vomit when she eats something she shouldn't have, and this is usually nothing to worry

87

about. However, if the vomitus looks bloody or otherwise unusual, call your vet immediately. If your dog has been throwing up, you may want to help her along to recovery by feeding a bland diet of rice with a little chicken. You may want to add a tablespoon of yogurt to help restore helpful microbes to the digestive tract.

Hereditary Problems of the West Highland White Terrier

Every breed of dog has some sort of breed or type-specific disorder. Some breeds are prone to more serious problems than others. However, none of this means that you must forego the pleasure of your chosen breed's companionship.

The West Highland White Terrier does present a number of health concerns, but in general this is a trouble-free breed and most Westies live to a ripe old age. You should spay or neuter your pet Westie anyway, but if any of these problems arise, you should alter your pet immediately if you haven't already. Affected dogs should *not* be bred.

SKIN DISEASES

Skin disease does occur in this breed. The Westie is a white, harsh-coated dog, and both these characteristics are conducive to skin troubles. The exact problem may not manifest itself until long after you have acquired your Westie. A skin disease is usually controllable by diet, medication, medicated baths or a combination of these. It happens occasionally that an affected dog must be put to sleep, but this is very rare. If your Westie is suffering from a skin disorder, you must find out exactly what problem you are dealing with.

Help is available. The West Highland White Terrier Club of America maintains a special task force called W.A.T.C.H., which is concerned with this and other aspects of Westie wellness. See Chapter 3 for getting in contact with the club directly on any matter of Westie health or any other question on the breed, or you can call W.A.T.C.H. at 508-564-4451.

ALLERGIES

Allergies happen in Westies, and many times they are the cause of skin problems. The only way to deal with a dog's allergies is to have sensitivity tests performed. Sometimes a Westie will have food allergies and must be fed a special diet. Other times a dog will be allergic to pollen or mold or other airborne irritants. Trees or flowers can be culprits, as can the carpet in your family room. For a well-loved family companion, it is not too much to have these tests done, and to keep the affected dog on a regimen of injections to help her lead a healthy, reasonably normal life.

CRANIO MANDIBULAR OSTEOPATHY

The bad news about CMO is that it is a painful inflammation of the lower jaw, causing difficulty in chewing and swallowing. The good news about the disease is that it is almost always seen in growing pup-pies and disappears by the time the dog is eight or nine months old. Treatment is with drugs dispensed by your veterinarian.

CMO, also knows as "lion jaw," is not seen until the puppy is several months old and probably in a new home.

Check your dog's teeth frequently and brush them regularly.

Even if your Westie's parents have a history of CMO, there is no way of knowing whether it will appear in their offspring or in which ones. If your Westie gets it, you should definitely tell the breeder about the situation.

LEGG-PERTHES' DISEASE

Legg-Perthes' disease is the necrotic degeneration of the femoral head. In plain English, that means that the head of the femur (the part of the upper hind-leg bone that fits into the pelvis) crumbles from a cutoff in the blood supply. This may be genetically trans-mitted, or it may be as a result of trauma. There is no documented proof to certify or disprove either claim.

Living with a
West Highland
White Terrier

Possibly, Legg-Perthes' can come from either cause. In any case, an affected dog will begin to limp and develop progressively less use of the affected leg. Treatment is via surgical removal of the damaged head and a conservative exercise regimen. Recovery is usually complete and rapid.

Legg-Perthes' disease is another condition that does not manifest itself until the puppy is more than six or seven months old, by which time most pet Westies will be in their new homes. The puppy's breeder may have had experience with Legg-Perthes', or this may be the first case. Regardless, let the breeder know about it.

LUXATING PATELLA

The patella is the kneecap and, in ordinary circumstances, it slides up and down in front of the knee joint. With a number of small breeds, including Westies, it will slide from its normal position toward the inner leg. The most obvious symptom is the onset of limping. A dog may or may not exhibit pain during these episodes. Luxating patella is a recurring condition that could eventually lead to arthritis; the only permanent cure is surgical correction of the affected knee. Sensible weight control and reasonable exercise levels will also benefit the affected individual.

DRY EYE

Science calls this disorder *keratitis sicca*, but whatever one calls it, it means the lack of production of tears. Obviously, this condition is very uncomfortable, and left untreated could cause permanent damage to the eye itself. Treatment consists of lubricating the eye with a number of daily applications of a special solution of "artificial tears" to keep the eye moist. One can also have surgery performed that involves resectioning the salivary glands. We had a Westie many years ago who developed dry eye, and we decided to have the surgery performed. Afterward, he developed prominent stains under his eyes because whenever he saw us eating anything, he would cry real tears!

Care of the Senior Citizen

Eventually your wonderful Westie is going to get old, as do we all. To ensure that she continues to enjoy a good quality of life, you can and should do a number of things to keep her both comfortable and happy during her senior years.

The Westie senior citizen will spend more time sleeping. She may not seem be as attentive to your comings and goings as she did when she was younger. She may walk more slowly with a few more halting steps than the hellion of a puppy you remember from a decade ago.

As a white, harsh-coated breed, the Westie can be prone to skin problems.

However, she is the reason you learned to love Westies, and she needs your love and loyalty now even more than she did when she was a puppy.

Make sure her bed is comfortable and located in a draft-free spot. Also remember that a Westie is never too old to be a busybody, so keep her bed where she can keep up with family activity. A small artificial lambskin rug would be especially appreciated on cold nights.

Now is a good time to talk to your veterinarian about your aging Westie's diet. Tell the vet what you are feeding when you bring her in for a checkup, and ask his or her advice about changing food.

Carefully monitor your Westie and groom her frequently. Just because the blush of youth is no longer upon her, don't neglect her appearance or her hygiene. Watch her teeth and keep them clean. If any appear broken or rotten, have them extracted. Your Westie will be happier and healthier as a result.

If you notice that your Westie has a persistent, unproductive cough, trot her into the doctor and have him or her listen to her heart. She may have the beginnings of congestive heart failure, a common condition in older dogs. Congestive heart failure can be effectively controlled with diuretic therapy. I'll bet you know a lot of older people who also take medication first thing in the morning. If they can, your Westie can!

Your senior Westie will still be a wonderful companion, though she may sleep more than she used to.

Make it a point to check your Westie's vision and hearing regularly. Cataracts are a common consequence of aging in dogs. Your Westie may lose all or part of her vision, but if you have her in familiar surroundings, she will probably get along just fine. Yes, surgery is available to remove cataracts, but you must also consider whether she is a good candidate for surgery and how much risk she will be exposed to as a result of the anesthetic. Again, your veterinarian is the best-qualified person to advise you on the best course of action.

A Westie who suffers complete or partial hearing loss needs you to protect her whenever she is out of the house. If she can't hear, she is less likely to react to any imminent danger.

Euthanasia

The likelihood of a well-loved old dog slipping peacefully away in her sleep is remote. Far more often, an old dog is brought to the veterinarian's office for euthanasia. Euthanasia (painless death) is a prospect every dog owner must face sooner or later. As I bring this section of the book to a close, I want to share my thought on the subject with you. It's important that you understand as much about the end of your dog's life as I hope you now do about the beginning and the middle.

The time to consider euthanasia for your dog is when her quality of life is no longer sufficient. Many owners are guilty of thinking more of their own feelings than their dogs' when they elect to delay the inevitable. Remember, your Westie has a sense of only the present and the past. She lives today and does not have a handle on the future. For her, the end of life holds no terrors.

When you must put your pet to sleep, she needs you to support her just as you did all her life. I know from experience that putting down a dog is not easy, and it never gets easier. I have often observed teary-eyed pet owners coming to the veterinarian's office, old dog in tow, only to leave their faithful friend to end her time on earth surrounded by strangers. Please don't ever do that to your Westie. Euthanasia is not painful, but an old dog's confusion can be terribly stressful. When the sedative is administered, show your dog the loyalty she has shown to you. Stay with her. Let yours be the last voice she hears. You'll be doing the right thing, and you owe it to your dog.

Another Westie

If yours was a one-Westie household, you will probably want another to fill the empty space left by your old friend. The time to seek a new Westie is for you to determine, but it is better to let a little time go by. This way, you give yourself a chance to heal from the loss of

Living with a
West Highland
White Terrier

your old pet and allow the newcomer to make her
own inroads on your heart in her own ways and for
her own reasons.

Ask any Westie lover whether life without "Colonel
Malcom's favorite" is worth living. After a little
thought, he or she is likely to tell you that it is, but
could never be the same as when an exuberant Westie
keeps telling you how much you mean to her.

Your Happy, Healthy Pet

Your Dog's Name _____

Name on Your Dog's Pedigree (if your dog has one) _____

_____

Where Your Dog Came From _____

_____

Your Dog's Birthday _____

Your Dog's Veterinarian

    Name _____

    Address _____

    Phone Number_____

    Emergency Number_____

Your Dog's Health

    Vaccines

    type _____ date given _____

    type _____ date given _____

    type _____ date given _____

    type _____ date given _____

    Heartworm

    date tested _____ type used_____ start date _____

Your Dog's License Number_____

Groomer's Name and Number _____

Dogsitter/Walker's Name and Number _____

Awards Your Dog Has Won

    Award _____ date earned _____

    Award _____ date earned _____

part three

Enjoying your Dog

chapter 8

Basic
Training

by Ian Dunbar, Ph.D., MRCVS

Training is the jewel in the crown—the most important aspect of doggy husbandry. There is no more important variable influencing dog behavior and temperament than the dog's education: A well-trained, well-behaved and good-natured puppydog is always a joy to live with, but an untrained and uncivilized dog can be a perpetual nightmare. Moreover, deny the dog an education and she will not have the opportunity to fulfill her own canine potential; neither will she have the ability to communicate effectively with her human companions.

Luckily, modern psychological training methods are easy, efficient, effective and, above all, considerably dog-friendly and user-friendly.

Doggy education is as simple as it is enjoyable. But before you can have a good time play-training with your new dog, you have to learn what to do and how to do it. There is no bigger variable influencing the success of dog training than the *owner's* experience and expertise. *Before you embark on the dog's education, you must first educate yourself.*

Basic Training for Owners

Ideally, basic owner training should begin well *before* you select your dog. Find out all you can about your chosen breed first, then master rudimentary training and handling skills. If you already have your puppy-dog, owner training is a dire emergency—the clock is ticking! Especially for puppies, the first few weeks at home are the most important and influential days in the dog's life. Indeed, the cause of most adolescent and adult problems may be traced back to the initial days the pup explores her new home. This is the time to establish the *status quo*—to teach the puppydog how you would like her to behave and so prevent otherwise quite predictable problems.

In addition to consulting breeders and breed books such as this one (which understandably have a positive breed bias), seek out as many pet owners with your breed as you can find. Good points are obvious. What you want to find out are the breed-specific *problems,* so you can nip them in the bud. In particular, you should talk to owners with *adolescent* dogs and make a list of all anticipated problems. Most important, *test drive* at least half a dozen adolescent and adult dogs of your breed yourself. An 8-week-old puppy is deceptively easy to handle, but she will acquire adult size, speed and strength in just four months, so you should learn now what to prepare for.

Puppy and pet dog training classes offer a convenient venue to locate pet owners and observe dogs in action. For a list of suitable trainers in your area, contact the Association of Pet Dog Trainers (see chapter 13). You may also begin your basic owner training by observing

other owners in class. Watch as many classes and test
drive as many dogs as possible. Select an upbeat, dog-
friendly, people-friendly, fun-and-games, puppydog pet
training class to learn the ropes. Also, watch training
videos and read training books. You must find out what
to do and how to do it *before* you have to do it.

Principles of Training

Most people think training comprises teaching the dog
to do things such as sit, speak and roll over, but even a
4-week-old pup knows how to do these things already.
Instead, the first step in training involves teaching
the dog human words for each dog behavior and activity and for each aspect of the dog's environment. That
way you, the owner, can more easily participate in the
dog's domestic education by directing her to perform
specific actions appropriately, that is, at the right time,
in the right place and so on. Training opens communication channels, enabling an educated dog to at least
understand her owner's requests.

In addition to teaching a dog *what* we want her to
do, it is also necessary to teach her *why* she should do
what we ask. Indeed, 95 percent of training revolves
around motivating the dog *to want to do* what we want.
Dogs often understand what their owners want; they
just don't see the point of doing it—especially when
the owner's repetitively boring and seemingly senseless
instructions are totally at odds with much more pressing and exciting doggy distractions. It is not so much
the dog that is being stubborn or dominant; rather, it
is the owner who has failed to acknowledge the dog's
needs and feelings and to approach training from the
dog's point of view.

THE MEANING OF INSTRUCTIONS

The secret to successful training is learning how to use
training lures to predict or prompt specific behaviors—
to coax the dog to do what you want *when* you want.
Any highly valued object (such as a treat or toy) may be
used as a lure, which the dog will follow with her eyes

and nose. Moving the lure in specific ways entices the dog to move her nose, head and entire body in specific ways. In fact, by learning the art of manipulating various lures, it is possible to teach the dog to assume virtually any body position and perform any action. Once you have control over the expression of the dog's behaviors and can elicit any body position or behavior at will, you can easily teach the dog to perform on request.

Teach your dog words for each activity she needs to know, like down.

Tell your dog what you want her to do, use a lure to entice her to respond correctly, then profusely praise and maybe reward her once she performs the desired action. For example, verbally request "Tina, sit!" while you move a squeaky toy upwards and backwards over the dog's muzzle (lure-movement and hand signal), smile knowingly as she looks up (to follow the lure) and sits down (as a result of canine anatomical engineering), then praise her to distraction ("Gooood Tina!"). Squeak the toy, offer a training treat and give your dog and yourself a pat on the back.

Being able to elicit desired responses over and over enables the owner to reward the dog over and over. Consequently, the dog begins to think training is fun. For example, the more the dog is rewarded for sitting, the more she enjoys sitting. Eventually the dog comes to realize that, whereas most sitting is appreciated, sitting immediately upon request usually prompts especially enthusiastic praise and a slew of high-level rewards. The dog begins to sit on cue much of the time, showing that she is starting to grasp the meaning of the owner's verbal request and hand signal.

WHY COMPLY?

Most dogs enjoy initial lure-reward training and are only too happy to comply with their owners' wishes. Unfortunately, repetitive drilling without appreciative feedback tends to diminish the dog's enthusiasm until she eventually fails to see the point of complying anymore. Moreover, as the dog approaches adolescence she becomes more easily distracted as she develops other interests. Lengthy sessions with repetitive exercises tend to bore and demotivate both parties. If it's not fun, the owner doesn't do it and neither does the dog.

Integrate training into your dog's life: The greater number of training sessions each day and the *shorter* they are, the more willingly compliant your dog will

become. Make sure to have a short (just a few seconds) training interlude before every enjoyable canine activity. For example, ask your dog to sit to greet people, to sit before you throw her Frisbee and to sit for her supper. Really, sitting is no different from a canine "Please."

To train your dog, you need gentle hands, a loving heart and a good attitude.

Also, include numerous short training interludes during every enjoyable canine pastime, for example, when playing with the dog or when she is running in the park. In this fashion, doggy distractions may be effectively converted into rewards for training. Just as all games have rules, fun becomes training . . . and training becomes fun.

Eventually, rewards actually become unnecessary to continue motivating your dog. If trained with consideration and kindness, performing the desired behaviors will become self-rewarding and, in a sense, your dog will motivate herself. Just as it is not necessary to reward a human companion during an enjoyable walk in the park, or following a game of tennis, it is hardly necessary to reward our best friend—the dog— for walking by our side or while playing fetch. Human company during enjoyable activities is reward enough for most dogs.

Even though your dog has become self-motivating, it's still good to praise and pet her a lot and offer rewards once in a while, especially for a good job well done. And if for no other reason, praising and rewarding others is good for the human heart.

PUNISHMENT

Without a doubt, lure-reward training is by far the best way to teach: Entice your dog to do what you want and then reward her for doing so. Unfortunately, a human shortcoming is to take the good for granted and to moan and groan at the bad. Specifically, the dog's many good behaviors are ignored while the owner focuses on punishing the dog for making mistakes. In extreme cases, instruction is *limited* to punishing mistakes made by a trainee dog, child, employee or husband, even though it has been proven punishment training is notoriously inefficient and ineffective and is decidedly unfriendly and combative. It teaches the dog that training is a drag, almost as quickly as it teaches the dog to dislike her trainer. Why treat our best friends like our worst enemies?

Punishment training is also much more laborious and time consuming. Whereas it takes only a finite amount of time to teach a dog what to chew, for example, it takes much, much longer to punish the dog for each and every mistake. Remember, *there is only one right way!* So why not teach that right way from the outset?!

Enjoying Your
Dog

To make matters worse, punishment training causes severe lapses in the dog's reliability. Since it is obviously impossible to punish the dog each and every time she misbehaves, the dog quickly learns to distinguish between those times when she must comply (so as to avoid impending punishment) and those times when she need not comply, because punishment is impossible. Such times include when the dog is off leash and 6 feet away, when the owner is otherwise engaged (talking to a friend, watching television, taking a shower, tending to the baby or chatting on the telephone) or when the dog is left at home alone.

Instances of misbehavior will be numerous when the owner is away, because even when the dog complied in the owner's looming presence, she did so unwillingly. The dog was forced to act against her will, rather than molding her will to want to please. Hence, when the owner is absent, not only does the dog know she need not comply, she simply does not want to. Again, the trainee is not a stubborn vindictive beast, but rather the trainer has failed to teach. Punishment training invariably creates unpredictable Jekyll and Hyde behavior.

Trainer's Tools

Many training books extol the virtues of a vast array of training paraphernalia and electronic and metallic gizmos, most of which are designed for canine restraint, correction and punishment, rather than for actual facilitation of doggy education. In reality, most effective training tools are not found in stores; they come from within ourselves. In addition to a willing dog, all you really need is a functional human brain, gentle hands, a loving heart and a good attitude.

In terms of equipment, all dogs do require a quality buckle collar to sport dog tags and to attach the leash (for safety and to comply with local leash laws). Hollow chew toys (like Kongs or sterilized longbones) and a dog bed or collapsible crate are musts for housetraining. Three additional tools are required:

1. specific lures (training treats and toys) to predict and prompt specific desired behaviors;

2. rewards (praise, affection, training treats and toys) to reinforce for the dog what a lot of fun it all is; and

3. knowledge—how to convert the dog's favorite activities and games (potential distractions to training) into "life-rewards," which may be employed to facilitate training.

The most powerful of these is *knowledge*. Education is the key! Watch training classes, participate in training classes, watch videos, read books, enjoy play-training with your dog and then your dog will say "Please," and your dog will say "Thank you!"

Housetraining

If dogs were left to their own devices, certainly they would chew, dig and bark for entertainment and then no doubt highlight a few areas of their living space with sprinkles of urine, in much the same way we decorate by hanging pictures. Consequently, when we ask a dog to live with us, we must teach her *where* she may dig, *where* she may perform her toilet duties, *what* she may chew and *when* she may bark. After all, when left at home alone for many hours, we cannot expect the dog to amuse herself by completing crosswords or watching the soaps on TV!

Also, it would be decidedly unfair to keep the house rules a secret from the dog, and then get angry and punish the poor critter for inevitably transgressing rules she did not even know existed. Remember: Without adequate education and guidance, the dog will be forced to establish her own rules—doggy rules—and most probably will be at odds with the owner's view of domestic living.

Since most problems develop during the first few days the dog is at home, prospective dog owners must be certain they are quite clear about the principles of housetraining *before* they get a dog. Early misbehaviors quickly become established as the *status quo*—

becoming firmly entrenched as hard-to-break bad habits, which set the precedent for years to come. Make sure to teach your dog good habits right from the start. Good habits are just as hard to break as bad ones!

Ideally, when a new dog comes home, try to arrange for someone to be present as much as possible during the first few days (for adult dogs) or weeks for puppies. With only a little forethought, it is surprisingly easy to find a puppy sitter, such as a retired person, who would be willing to eat from your refrigerator and watch your television while keeping an eye on the newcomer to encourage the dog to play with chew toys and to ensure she goes outside on a regular basis.

POTTY TRAINING

To teach the dog where to relieve herself:

1. never let her make a single mistake;
2. let her know where you want her to go; and
3. handsomely reward her for doing so: "GOOOOOOOD DOG!!!" liver treat, liver treat, liver treat!

Preventing Mistakes

A single mistake is a training disaster, since it heralds many more in future weeks. And each time the dog soils the house, this further reinforces the dog's unfortunate preference for an indoor, carpeted toilet. *Do not let an unhousetrained dog have full run of the house.*

When you are away from home, or cannot pay full attention, confine the dog to an area where elimination is appropriate, such as an outdoor run or, better still, a small, comfortable indoor kennel with access to an outdoor run. When confined in this manner, most dogs will naturally housetrain themselves.

If that's not possible, confine the dog to an area, such as a utility room, kitchen, basement or garage, where elimination may not be desired in the long run but as an interim measure it is certainly preferable to doing it all around the house. Use newspaper to cover the floor of the dog's day room. The newspaper may be used to soak up the urine and to wrap up and dispose of the feces. Once your dog develops a preferred spot for eliminating, it is only necessary to cover that part of the floor with newspaper. The smaller papered area may then be moved (only a little each day) towards the door to the outside. Thus the dog will develop the tendency to go to the door when she needs to relieve herself.

Never confine an unhousetrained dog to a crate for long periods. Doing so would force the dog to soil the crate and ruin its usefulness as an aid for housetraining (see the following discussion).

Teaching Where

In order to teach your dog where you would like her to do her business, you have to be there to direct the proceedings—an obvious, yet often neglected, fact of life. In order to be there to teach the dog *where* to go, you need to know *when* she needs to go. Indeed, the success of housetraining depends on the owner's ability to predict these times. Certainly, a regular feeding schedule will facilitate prediction somewhat, but there is nothing like "loading the deck" and influencing the timing of the outcome yourself!

The first few weeks at home are the most important and influential in your dog's life.

Whenever you are at home, make sure the dog is under constant supervision and/or confined to a small

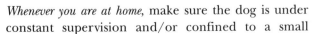

area. If already well trained, simply instruct the dog to lie down in her bed or basket. Alternatively, confine the dog to a crate (doggy den) or tie-down (a short, 18-inch lead that can be clipped to an eye hook in the baseboard near her bed). Short-term close confinement strongly inhibits urination and defecation, since the dog does not want to soil her sleeping area. Thus, when you release the puppydog each hour, she will definitely need to urinate immediately and defecate every third or fourth hour. Keep the dog confined to her doggy den and take her to her intended toilet area each hour, every hour and on the hour.

When taking your dog outside, instruct her to sit quietly before opening the door—she will soon learn to sit by the door when she needs to go out!

Teaching Why

Being able to predict when the dog needs to go enables the owner to be on the spot to praise and reward the dog. Each hour, hurry the dog to the intended toilet area in the yard, issue the appropriate instruction ("Go pee!" or "Go poop!"), then give the dog three to four minutes to produce. Praise and offer a couple of training treats when successful. The treats are important because many people fail to praise their dogs with feeling . . . and housetraining is hardly the time for understatement. So either loosen up and enthusiastically praise that dog: "Wuzzzer-wuzzer-wuzzer, hoooser good wuffer den? Hoooo went pee for Daddy?" Or say "Good dog!" as best you can and offer the treats for effect.

Following elimination is an ideal time for a spot of play-training in the yard or house. Also, an empty dog may be allowed greater freedom around the house for the next half hour or so, just as long as you keep an eye out to make sure she does not get into other kinds of mischief. If you are preoccupied and cannot pay full attention, confine the dog to her doggy den once more to enjoy a peaceful snooze or to play with her many chew toys.

If your dog does not eliminate within the allotted time outside—no biggie! Back to her doggy den, and then try again after another hour.

As I own large dogs, I always feel more relaxed walking an empty dog, knowing that I will not need to finish our stroll weighted down with bags of feces!

Beware of falling into the trap of walking the dog to get her to eliminate. The good ol' dog walk is such an enormous highlight in the dog's life that it represents the single biggest potential reward in domestic dogdom. However, when in a hurry, or during inclement weather, many owners abruptly terminate the walk the moment the dog has done her business. This, in effect, severely punishes the dog for doing the right thing, in the right place at the right time. Consequently, many dogs become strongly inhibited from eliminating outdoors because they know it will signal an abrupt end to an otherwise thoroughly enjoyable walk.

Instead, instruct the dog to relieve herself in the yard prior to going for a walk. If you follow the above instructions, most dogs soon learn to eliminate on cue. As soon as the dog eliminates, praise (and offer a treat or two)—"Good dog! Let's go walkies!" Use the walk as a reward for eliminating in the yard. If the dog does not go, put her back in her doggy den and think about a walk later on. You will find with a "No feces—no walk" policy, your dog will become one of the fastest defecators in the business.

If you do not have a backyard, instruct the dog to eliminate right outside your front door prior to the walk. Not only will this facilitate clean up and disposal of the feces in your own trash can but, also, the walk may again be used as a colossal reward.

CHEWING AND BARKING

Short-term close confinement also teaches the dog that occasional quiet moments are a reality of domestic living. Your puppydog is extremely impressionable during her first few weeks at home. Regular confinement at this time soon exerts a calming influence over the dog's personality. Remember, once the dog is housetrained and calmer, there will be a whole lifetime ahead for the dog to enjoy full run of the house and garden. On the other hand, by letting the newcomer have unrestricted access to the entire household and allowing her to run willy-nilly, she will most certainly develop a bunch of behavior problems in short order, no doubt necessitating confinement later in life. It would not be fair to remedially restrain and confine a dog you have trained, through neglect, to run free.

When confining the dog, make sure she always has an impressive array of suitable chew toys. Kongs and sterilized longbones (both readily available from pet stores) make the best chew toys, since they are hollow and may be stuffed with treats to heighten the dog's interest. For example, by stuffing the little hole at the top of a Kong with a small piece of freeze-dried liver, the dog will not want to leave it alone.

Remember, treats do not have to be junk food and they certainly should not represent extra calories. Rather, treats should be part of each dog's regular

Make sure your puppy has suitable chew toys.

daily diet: Some food may be served in the dog's bowl for breakfast and dinner, some food may be used as training treats, and some food may be used for stuffing chew toys. I regularly stuff my dogs' many Kongs with different shaped biscuits and kibble. The kibble seems to fall out fairly easily, as do the oval-shaped biscuits, thus rewarding the dog instantaneously for checking out the chew toys. The bone-shaped biscuits fall out after a while, rewarding the dog for worrying at the chew toy. But the triangular biscuits never come out. They remain inside the Kong as lures, maintaining the dog's fascination with her chew toy. To further focus the dog's interest, I always make sure to flavor the triangular biscuits by rubbing them with a little cheese or freeze-dried liver.

To teach come, call your dog, open your arms as a welcoming signal, wave a toy or a treat and praise for every step in your direction.

If stuffed chew toys are reserved especially for times the dog is confined, the puppydog will soon learn to enjoy quiet moments in her doggy den and she will quickly develop a chew-toy habit— a good habit! This is a simple *autoshaping* process; all the owner has to do is set up the situation and the dog all but trains herself— easy and effective. Even when the dog is given run of the house, her first inclination will be to indulge her rewarding chew-toy habit rather than destroy less-attractive household articles, such as curtains, carpets, chairs and compact disks. Similarly, a chew-toy chewer will be less inclined to scratch and chew herself excessively. Also, if the dog busies herself as a recreational chewer, she will be less inclined to develop into a recreational barker or digger when left at home alone.

Stuff a number of chew toys whenever the dog is left confined and remove the extra-special-tasting treats when you return. Your dog will now amuse herself with her chew toys before falling asleep and then resume playing with her chew toys when she expects you to return. Since most owner-absent misbehavior happens right after you leave and right before your expected return, your puppydog will now be conveniently preoccupied with her chew toys at these times.

Come and Sit

Most puppies will happily approach virtually anyone, whether called or not; that is, until they collide with adolescence and develop other more important doggy interests, such as sniffing a multiplicity of exquisite odors on the grass. Your mission, Mr./Ms. Owner, is to teach and reward the pup for coming reliably, willingly and happily when called—and you have just three months to get it done. Unless adequately reinforced, your puppy's tendency to approach people will self-destruct by adolescence.

Call your dog ("Tina, come!"), open your arms (and maybe squat down) as a welcoming signal, waggle a treat or toy as a lure and reward the puppydog when she comes running. Do not wait to praise the dog until she reaches you—she may come 95 percent of the way and then run off after some distraction. Instead, praise the dog's *first* step towards you and continue praising enthusiastically for *every* step she takes in your direction.

When the rapidly approaching puppy dog is three lengths away from impact, instruct her to sit ("Tina, sit!") and hold the lure in front of you in an outstretched hand to prevent her from hitting you mid-chest and knocking you flat on your back! As Tina decelerates to nose the lure, move the treat upwards and backwards just over her muzzle with an upwards motion of your extended arm (palm-upwards). As the dog looks up to follow the lure, she will sit down (if she jumps up, you are holding the lure too high). Praise the dog for sitting. Move backwards and call her again. Repeat this many times over, always praising when Tina comes and sits; on occasion, reward her.

For the first couple of trials, use a training treat both as a lure to entice the dog to come and sit and as a reward for doing so. Thereafter, try to use different items as lures and rewards. For example, lure the dog with a Kong or Frisbee but reward her with a food treat. Or lure the dog with a food treat but pat her and throw a tennis ball as a reward. After just a few repetitions, dispense with the lures and rewards; the dog will begin to respond willingly to your verbal requests and hand signals just for the prospect of praise from your heart and affection from your hands.

Instruct every family member, friend and visitor how to get the dog to come and sit. Invite people over for a series of pooch parties; do not keep the pup a secret—let other people enjoy this puppy, and let the pup enjoy other people. Puppydog parties are not only fun, they easily attract a lot of people to help *you* train *your* dog. Unless you teach your dog how to meet people, that is, to sit for greetings, no doubt the dog will resort to jumping up. Then you and the visitors will get annoyed, and the dog will be punished. This is not fair. *Send out those invitations for puppy parties and teach your dog to be mannerly and socially acceptable.*

Even though your dog quickly masters obedient recalls in the house, her reliability may falter when playing in the backyard or local park. Ironically, it is *the owner* who has unintentionally trained the dog *not* to respond in these instances. By allowing the dog to play and run around and otherwise have a good time, but then to call the dog to put her on leash to take her home, the dog quickly learns playing is fun but training is a drag. Thus, playing in the park becomes a severe distraction, which works against training. Bad news!

Instead, whether playing with the dog off leash or on leash, request her to come at frequent intervals—say, every minute or so. On most occasions, praise and pet the dog for a few seconds while she is sitting, then tell her to go play again. For especially fast recalls, offer a couple of training treats and take the time to praise and pet the dog enthusiastically before releasing her. The dog will learn that coming when called is not necessarily the end of the play session, and neither is it the end of the world; rather, it signals an enjoyable, quality time-out with the owner before resuming play once more. In fact, playing in the park now becomes a very effective life-reward, which works to facilitate training by reinforcing each obedient and timely recall. Good news!

Sit, Down, Stand and Rollover

Teaching the dog a variety of body positions is easy for owner and dog, impressive for spectators and extremely useful for all. Using lure-reward techniques, it is possible to train several positions at once to verbal commands or hand signals (which impress the socks off onlookers).

Sit and **down**—the two control commands—prevent or resolve nearly a hundred behavior problems. For example, if the dog happily and obediently sits or lies down when requested, she cannot jump on visitors, dash out the front door, run around and chase her tail, pester other dogs, harass cats or annoy family, friends or strangers. Additionally, "Sit" or "Down" are the best emergency commands for off-leash control.

It is easier to teach and maintain a reliable sit than maintain a reliable recall. *Sit* is the purest and simplest of commands—either the dog is sitting or she is not. If there is any change of circumstances or potential danger in the park, for example, simply instruct the dog to sit. If she sits, you have a number of options: Allow the dog to resume playing when she is safe, walk up and put the dog on leash or call the dog. The dog will be much more likely to come when called if she has already acknowledged her compliance by sitting. If the dog does not sit in the park—train her to!

Stand and **rollover-stay** are the two positions for examining the dog. Your veterinarian will love you to distraction if you take a little time to teach the dog to stand still and roll over and play possum. Also, your vet bills will be smaller because it will take the veterinarian less time to examine your dog. The rollover-stay is an especially useful command and is really just a variation of the down-stay: Whereas the dog lies prone in the traditional down, she lies supine in the rollover-stay.

As with teaching come and sit, the training techniques to teach the dog to assume all other body positions on cue are user-friendly and dog-friendly. Simply give the appropriate request, lure the dog into the desired body position using a training treat or toy and then *praise* (and maybe reward) the dog as soon as she complies. Try not to touch the dog to get her to respond. If you teach the dog by guiding her into position, the dog will quickly learn that rump-pressure means sit, for example, but as yet you still have no control over your dog if she is just 6 feet away. It will still be necessary to teach the dog to sit on request. So do not make training a time-consuming two-step process; instead, teach the dog to sit to a verbal request or hand signal from the outset. Once the dog sits willingly when requested, by all means use your hands to pet the dog when she does so.

To teach **down** when the dog is already sitting, say "Tina, down!," hold the lure in one hand (palm down) and lower that hand to the floor between the dog's forepaws. As the dog lowers her head to follow the lure, slowly move the lure away from the dog just a fraction (in front of her paws). The dog will lie down as she stretches her nose forward to follow the lure. Praise the dog when she does so. If the dog stands up, you pulled the lure away too far and too quickly.

When teaching the dog to lie down from the standing position, say "Down" and lower the lure to the floor as before. Once the dog has lowered her forequarters and assumed a play bow, gently and slowly move the lure *towards* the dog between her forelegs. Praise the dog as soon as her rear end plops down.

After just a couple of trials it will be possible to alternate sits and downs and have the dog energetically perform doggy push-ups. Praise the dog a lot, and after half a dozen or so push-ups reward the dog with a training treat or toy. You will notice the more energetically you move your arm—upwards (palm up) to get the dog to sit, and downwards (palm down) to get the dog to lie down—the more energetically the dog responds to your requests. Now try training the dog in silence and you will notice she has also learned to respond to hand signals. Yeah! Not too shabby for the first session.

To teach **stand** from the sitting position, say "Tina, stand," slowly move the lure half a dog-length away from the dog's nose, keeping it at nose level, and praise the dog as she stands to follow the lure. As soon

Using a food lure to teach sit, down and stand. 1) "Phoenix, sit." 2) Hand palm upwards, move lure up and back over dog's muzzle. 3) "Good sit, Phoenix!" 4) "Phoenix, down." 5) Hand palm downwards, move lure down to lie between dog's forepaws. 6) "Phoenix, off. Good down, Phoenix!" 7) "Phoenix, sit!" 8) Palm upwards, move lure up and back, keeping it close to dog's muzzle. 9) "Good sit, Phoenix!"

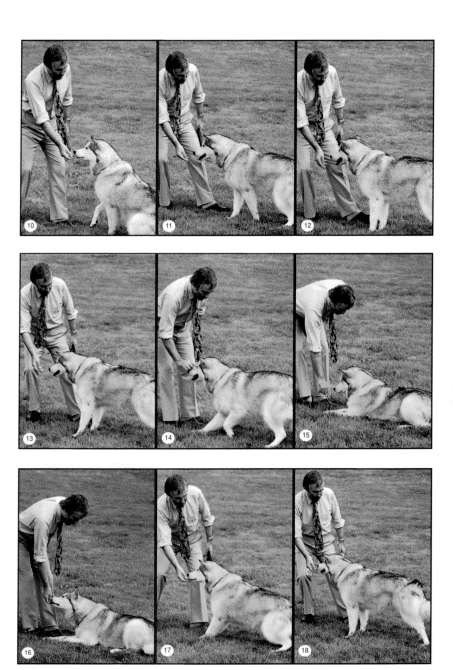

10) "Phoenix, stand!" 11) Move lure away from dog at nose height, then lower it a tad. 12) "Phoenix, off! Good stand, Phoenix!" 13) "Phoenix, down!" 14) Hand palm downwards, move lure down to lie between dog's forepaws. 15) "Phoenix, off! Good down-stay, Phoenix!" 16) "Phoenix, stand!" 17) Move lure away from dog's muzzle up to nose height. 18) "Phoenix, off! Good stand-stay, Phoenix. Now we'll make the vet and groomer happy!"

as the dog stands, lower the lure to just beneath the dog's chin to entice her to look down; otherwise she will stand and then sit immediately. To prompt the dog to stand from the down position, move the lure half a dog-length upwards and away from the dog, holding the lure at standing nose height from the floor.

Teaching *rollover* is best started from the down position, with the dog lying on one side, or at least with both hind legs stretched out on the same side. Say "Tina, bang!" and move the lure backwards and alongside the dog's muzzle to her elbow (on the side of her outstretched hind legs). Once the dog looks to the side and backwards, very slowly move the lure upwards to the dog's shoulder and backbone. Tickling the dog in the goolies (groin area) often invokes a reflex-raising of the hind leg as an appeasement gesture, which facilitates the tendency to roll over. If you move the lure too quickly and the dog jumps into the standing position, have patience and start again. As soon as the dog rolls onto her back, keep the lure stationary and mesmerize the dog with a relaxing tummy rub.

To teach *rollover-stay* when the dog is standing or moving, say "Tina, bang!" and give the appropriate hand signal (with index finger pointed and thumb cocked in true Sam Spade fashion), then in one fluid movement lure her to first lie down and then rollover-stay as above.

Teaching the dog to *stay* in each of the above four positions becomes a piece of cake after first teaching the dog not to worry at the toy or treat training lure. This is best accomplished by hand feeding dinner kibble. Hold a piece of kibble firmly in your hand and softly instruct "Off!" Ignore any licking and slobbering *for however long the dog worries at the treat*, but say "Take it!" and offer the kibble *the instant* the dog breaks contact with her muzzle. Repeat this a few times, and then up the ante and insist the dog remove her muzzle for one whole second before offering the kibble. Then progressively refine your criteria and have the dog not touch your hand (or treat) for longer and longer periods on each trial, such as for two seconds, four seconds, then six, ten, fifteen, twenty, thirty seconds and so on.

The dog soon learns: (1) worrying at the treat never gets results, whereas (2) noncontact is often rewarded after a variable time lapse.

Teaching *"Off!"* has many useful applications in its own right. Additionally, instructing the dog not to touch a training lure often produces spontaneous and magical stays. Request the dog to stand-stay, for example, and not to touch the lure. At first set your sights on a short two-second stay before rewarding the dog. (Remember, every long journey begins with a single step.) However, on subsequent trials, gradually and progressively increase the length of stay required to receive a reward. In no time at all your dog will stand calmly for a minute or so.

Relevancy Training

Once you have taught the dog what you expect her to do when requested to come, sit, lie down, stand, rollover and stay, the time is right to teach the dog *why* she should comply with your wishes. The secret is to have many (*many*) extremely short training interludes (two to five seconds each) at numerous (*numerous*) times during the course of the dog's day. Especially work with the dog immediately *before* the dog's good times and *during* the dog's good times. For example, ask your dog to sit and/or lie down each time before opening doors, serving meals, offering treats and tummy rubs; ask the dog to perform a few controlled doggy push-ups before letting her off leash or throwing a tennis ball; and perhaps request the dog to sit-down-sit-stand-down-stand-rollover before inviting her to cuddle on the couch.

Similarly, request the dog to sit many times during play or on walks, and in no time at all the dog will be only too pleased to follow your instructions because she has learned that a compliant response heralds all sorts of goodies. Basically all you are trying to teach the dog is how to say please: "Please throw the tennis ball. Please may I snuggle on the couch."

Remember, it is important to keep training interludes short and to have many short sessions each and every day. The shortest (and most useful) session comprises asking the dog to sit and then go play during a play session. When trained this way, your dog will soon associate training with good times. In fact, the dog may be unable to distinguish between training and good times and, indeed, there should be no distinction. The warped concept that training involves forcing the dog to comply and/or dominating her will is totally at odds with the picture of a truly well-trained dog. In reality, enjoying a game of training with a dog is no different from enjoying a game of backgammon or tennis with a friend; and walking with a dog should be no different from strolling with a spouse, or with buddies on the golf course.

Walk by Your Side

Many people attempt to teach a dog to heel by putting her on a leash and physically correcting the dog when she makes mistakes. There are a number of things seriously wrong with this approach, the first being that most people do not want precision heeling; rather, they simply want the dog to follow or walk by their side. Second, when physically restrained during "training," even though the dog may grudgingly mope by your side when "handcuffed" on leash, let's see what happens when she is off leash. History! The dog is in the next county because she never enjoyed walking with you on leash and you have no control over her off leash. So let's just teach the dog off leash from the outset to *want* to walk with us. Third, if the dog has not been trained to heel, it is a trifle hasty to think about punishing the poor dog for making mistakes and breaking heeling rules she didn't even know existed. This is simply not fair! Surely, if the dog had been adequately taught how to heel, she would seldom make mistakes and hence there would be no need to correct the dog. Remember, each mistake and each correction (punishment) advertise the trainer's inadequacy, not the dog's. The dog is not stubborn, she is not stupid and she is not bad. Even if she were, she would still require training, so let's train her properly.

Let's teach the dog to *enjoy* following us and to *want* to walk by our side off leash. Then it will be easier to teach high-precision off-leash heeling patterns if desired. Before going on outdoor walks, it is necessary to teach the dog not to pull. Then it becomes easy to teach on-leash walking and heeling because the dog already wants to walk with you, she is familiar with the desired walking and heeling positions and she knows not to pull.

FOLLOWING

Start by training your dog to follow you. Many puppies will follow if you simply walk away from them and maybe click your fingers or chuckle. Adult dogs may require additional enticement to stimulate them to follow, such as a training lure or, at the very least, a lively trainer. To teach the dog to follow: (1) keep walking and (2) walk away from the dog. If the dog attempts to lead or lag, change pace; slow down if the dog forges too far ahead, but speed up if she lags too far behind. Say "Steady!" or "Easy!" each time before you slow down and "Quickly!" or "Hustle!" each time before you speed up, and the dog will learn to change pace on cue. If the dog lags or leads too far, or if she wanders right or left, simply walk quickly in the opposite direction and maybe even run away from the dog and hide.

Practicing is a lot of fun; you can set up a course in your home, yard or park to do this. Indoors, entice the dog to follow upstairs, into a bedroom, into the bathroom, downstairs, around the living room couch, zigzagging between dining room chairs and into the kitchen for dinner. Outdoors, get the dog to follow around park benches, trees, shrubs and along walkways and lines in the grass. (For safety outdoors, it is advisable to attach a long line on the dog, but never exert corrective tension on the line.)

121

Remember, following has a lot to do with attitude—
your attitude! Most probably your dog will *not* want to
follow Mr. Grumpy Troll with the personality of wilted
lettuce. Lighten up—walk with a jaunty step, whistle a
happy tune, sing, skip and tell jokes to your dog and
she will be right there by your side.

BY YOUR SIDE

It is smart to train the dog to walk close on one side or
the other—either side will do, your choice. When walking, jogging or cycling, it is generally bad news to have
the dog suddenly cut in front of you. In fact, I train my
dogs to walk "By my side" and "Other side"—both very
useful instructions. It is possible to position the dog
fairly accurately by looking to the appropriate side and
clicking your fingers or slapping your thigh on that
side. A precise positioning may be attained by holding
a training lure, such as a chew toy, tennis ball or food
treat. Stop and stand still several times throughout the
walk, just as you would when window shopping or
meeting a friend. Use the lure to make sure the dog
slows down and stays close whenever you stop.

When teaching the dog to heel, we generally want
her to sit in heel position when we stop. Teach heel

*Using a toy to teach sit-heel-sit sequences: 1) "Phoenix, sit!" Standing still, move lure up and back over dog's
muzzle . . . 2) to position dog sitting in heel position on your left side. 3) Say "Phoenix, heel!" and walk ahead,
wagging lure in left hand. Change lure to right hand in preparation for sit signal. Say "Sit" and then . . .*

position at the standstill and the dog will learn that the default heel position is sitting by your side (left or right—your choice, unless you wish to compete in obedience trials, in which case the dog must heel on the left).

Several times a day, stand up and call your dog to come and sit in heel position—"Tina, heel!" For example, instruct the dog to come to heel each time there are commercials on TV, or each time you turn a page of a novel, and the dog will get it in a single evening.

Practice straight-line heeling and turns separately. With the dog sitting at heel, teach her to turn in place. After each quarter-turn, half-turn or full turn in place, lure the dog to sit at heel. Now it's time for short straight-line heeling sequences, no more than a few steps at a time. Always think of heeling in terms of sit-heel-sit sequences—start and end with the dog in position and do your best to keep her there when moving. Progressively increase the number of steps in each sequence. When the dog remains close for 20 yards of straight-line heeling, it is time to add a few turns and then sign up for a happy-heeling obedience class to get some advice from the experts.

4) use hand signal to lure dog to sit as you stop. Eventually, dog will sit automatically at heel whenever you stop. 5) "Good dog!"

No Pulling on Leash

You can start teaching your dog not to pull on leash anywhere—in front of the television or outdoors—but regardless of location, you must not take a single step with tension in the leash. For a reason known only to dogs, even just a couple of paces of pulling on leash is intrinsically motivating and diabolically rewarding. Instead, attach the leash to the dog's collar, grasp the other end firmly with both hands held close to your chest, and stand still—do not budge an inch. Have somebody watch you with a stopwatch to time your progress, or else you will never believe this will work and so you will not even try the exercise, and your shoulder and the dog's neck will be traumatized for years to come.

Stand still and wait for the dog to stop pulling, and to sit and/or lie down. All dogs stop pulling and sit eventually. Most take only a couple of minutes; the all-time record is 22½ minutes. Time how long it takes. Gently praise the dog when she stops pulling, and as soon as she sits, enthusiastically praise the dog and take just one step forward, then immediately stand still. This single step usually demonstrates the ballistic reinforcing nature of pulling on leash; most dogs explode to the end of the leash, so be prepared for the strain. Stand firm and wait for the dog to sit again. Repeat this half a dozen times and you will probably notice a progressive reduction in the force of the dog's one-step explosions and a radical reduction in the time it takes for the dog to sit each time.

As the dog learns "Sit we go" and "Pull we stop," she will begin to walk forward calmly with each single step and automatically sit when you stop. Now try two steps before you stop. Wooooooo! Scary! When the dog has mastered two steps at a time, try for three. After each success, progressively increase the number of steps in the sequence: try four steps and then six, eight, ten and twenty steps before stopping. Congratulations! You are now walking the dog on leash.

Whenever walking with the dog (off leash or on leash), make sure you stop periodically to practice a few position commands and stays before instructing the dog to "Walk on!" (Remember, you want the dog to be compliant everywhere, not just in the kitchen when her dinner is at hand.) For example, stopping every 25 yards to briefly train the dog amounts to over 200 training interludes within a single 3-mile stroll. And each training session is in a different location. You will not believe the improvement within just the first mile of the first walk.

To put it another way, integrating training into a walk offers 200 separate opportunities to use the continuance of the walk as a reward to reinforce the dog's education. Moreover, some training interludes may comprise continuing education for the dog's walking skills: Alternate short periods of the dog walking calmly by your side with periods when the dog is allowed to sniff and investigate the environment. Now sniffing odors on the grass and meeting other dogs become rewards which reinforce the dog's calm and mannerly demeanor. Good Lord! Whatever next? Many enjoyable walks together of course. Happy trails!

THE IMPORTANCE OF TRICKS

Nothing will improve a dog's quality of life better than having a few tricks under her belt. Teaching any trick expands the dog's vocabulary, which facilitates communication and improves the owner's control. Also, specific tricks help prevent and resolve specific behavior problems. For example, by teaching the dog to fetch her toys, the dog learns carrying a toy makes the owner happy and, therefore, will be more likely to chew her toy than other inappropriate items.

More important, teaching tricks prompts owners to lighten up and train with a sunny disposition. Really, tricks should be no different from any other behaviors we put on cue. But they are. When teaching tricks, owners have a much sweeter attitude, which in turn motivates the dog and improves her willingness to comply. The dog feels tricks are a blast, but formal commands are a drag. In fact, tricks are so enjoyable, they may be used as rewards in training by asking the dog to come, sit and down-stay and then rollover for a tummy rub. Go on, try it: Crack a smile and even giggle when the dog promptly and willingly lies down and stays.

Most important, performing tricks prompts onlookers to smile and giggle. Many people are scared of dogs, especially large ones. And nothing can be more off-putting for a dog than to be constantly confronted by strangers who don't like her because of her size or the way she looks. Uneasy people put the dog on edge, causing her to back off and bark, only frightening people all the more. And so a vicious circle develops, with the people's fear fueling the dog's fear *and vice versa*. Instead, tie a pink ribbon to your dog's collar and practice all sorts of tricks on walks and in the park, and you will be pleasantly amazed how it changes people's attitudes toward your friendly dog. The dog's repertoire of tricks is limited only by the trainer's imagination. Below I have described three of my favorites:

SPEAK AND SHUSH

The training sequence involved in teaching a dog to bark on request is no different from that used when training any behavior on cue: request—lure—response—reward. As always, the secret of success lies in finding an effective lure. If the dog always barks at the doorbell, for example, say "Rover, speak!", have an accomplice ring the doorbell, then reward the dog for barking. After a few woofs, ask Rover to "Shush!", waggle a food treat under her nose (to entice her to sniff and thus to shush), praise her when quiet and eventually offer the treat as a reward. Alternate "Speak" and "Shush," progressively increasing the length of shush-time between each barking bout.

PLAY BOW

With the dog standing, say "Bow!" and lower the food lure (palm upwards) to rest between the dog's forepaws. Praise as the dog lowers her forequarters and sternum to the ground (as when teaching the down), but then lure the dog to stand and offer the treat. On successive trials, gradually increase the length of time the dog is required to remain in the play bow posture in order to gain a food reward. If the dog's rear end collapses into a down, say nothing and offer no reward; simply start over.

BE A BEAR

With the dog sitting backed into a corner to prevent her from toppling over backwards, say "Be a bear!" With bent paw and palm down, raise a lure upwards and backwards along the top of the dog's muzzle. Praise the dog when she sits up on her haunches and offer the treat as a reward. To prevent the dog from standing on her hind legs, keep the lure closer to the dog's muzzle. On each trial, progressively increase the length of time the dog is required to sit up to receive a food reward. Since lure-reward training is so easy, teach the dog to stand and walk on her hind legs as well!

Teaching "Be a Bear"

chapter 9

Getting **Active** with your Dog

by Bardi McLennan

Once you and your dog have graduated from basic obedience training and are beginning to work together as a team, you can take part in the growing world of dog activities. There are so many fun things to do with your dog! Just remember, people and dogs don't always learn at the same pace, so don't be upset if you (or your dog) need more than two basic training courses before your team becomes operational. Even smart dogs don't go straight to college from kindergarten!

Just as there are events geared to certain types of dogs, so there are ones that are more appealing to certain types of people. In some activities, you give the commands and your dog does the work (upland game hunting is one example), while in others, such as agility, you'll both get a workout. You may want to aim for prestigious titles to add to your dog's name, or you may want nothing more than the sheer enjoyment of being around other people and their dogs. Passive or active, participation has its own rewards.

Consider your dog's physical capabilities when looking into any of the canine activities. It's easy to see that a Basset Hound is not built for the racetrack, nor would a Chihuahua be the breed of choice for pulling a sled. A loyal dog will attempt almost anything you ask him to do, so it is up to you to know your dog's limitations.

All dogs seem to love playing flyball.

A dog must be physically sound in order to compete at any level in athletic activities, and being mentally sound is a definite plus. Advanced age, however, may not be a deterrent. Many dogs still hunt and herd at ten or twelve years of age. It's entirely possible for dogs to be "fit at 50." Take your dog for a checkup, explain to your vet the type of activity you have in mind and be guided by his or her findings.

You needn't be restricted to breed-specific sports if it's only fun you're after. Certain AKC activities are limited to designated breeds; however, as each new trial, test or sport has grown in popularity, so has the variety of breeds encouraged to participate at a fun level.

But don't shortchange your fun, or that of your dog, by thinking only of the basic function of her breed. Once a dog has learned how to learn, she can be taught to do just about anything as long as the size of the dog is right for the job and you both think it is fun and rewarding. In other words, you are a team.

To get involved in any of the activities detailed in this chapter, look for the names and addresses of the organizations that sponsor them in Chapter 13. You can also ask your breeder or a local dog trainer for contacts.

You can compete in obedience trials with a well trained dog.

Official American Kennel Club Activities

The following tests and trials are some of the events sanctioned by the AKC and sponsored by various dog clubs. Your dog's expertise will be rewarded with impressive titles. You can participate just for fun, or be competitive and go for those awards.

OBEDIENCE

Training classes begin with pups as young as three months of age in kindergarten puppy training, then advance to pre-novice (all exercises on lead) and go on to novice, which is where you'll start off-lead work. In obedience classes dogs learn to sit, stay, heel and come through a variety of exercises. Once you've got the basics down, you can enter obedience trials and work toward earning your dog's first degree, a C.D. (Companion Dog).

The next level is called "Open," in which jumps and retrieves perk up the dog's interest. Passing grades in competition at this level earn a C.D.X. (Companion Dog Excellent). Beyond that lies the goal of the most ambitious—Utility (U.D. and even U.D.X. or OTCh, an Obedience Champion).

AGILITY

All dogs can participate in the latest canine sport to have gained worldwide popularity for its fun and excitement, agility. It began in England as a canine version of horse show-jumping, but because dogs are more agile and able to perform on verbal commands, extra feats were added such as climbing, balancing and racing through tunnels or in and out of weave poles. Many of the obstacles (regulation or homemade) can be set up in your own backyard. If the agility bug bites, you could end up in international competition!

For starters, your dog should be obedience trained, even though, in the beginning, the lessons may all be taught on lead. Once the dog understands the commands (and you do, too), it's as easy as guiding the dog over a prescribed course, one obstacle at a time. In competition, the race is against the clock, so wear your running shoes! The dog starts with 200 points and the judge deducts for infractions and misadventures along the way.

All dogs seem to love agility and respond to it as if they were being turned loose in a playground paradise. Your dog's enthusiasm will be contagious; agility turns into great fun for dog and owner.

FIELD TRIALS AND HUNTING TESTS

There are field trials and hunting tests for the sporting breeds—retrievers, spaniels and pointing breeds, and for some hounds—Bassets, Beagles and Dachshunds. Field trials are competitive events that test a dog's ability to perform the functions for which she was bred. Hunting tests, which are open to retrievers,

---

TITLES AWARDED BY THE AKC

Conformation: Ch. (Champion)

Obedience: CD (Companion Dog); CDX (Companion Dog Excellent); UD (Utility Dog); UDX (Utility Dog Excellent); OTCh. (Obedience Trial Champion)

Field: JH (Junior Hunter); SH (Senior Hunter); MH (Master Hunter); AFCh. (Amateur Field Champion); FCh. (Field Champion)

Lure Coursing: JC (Junior Courser); SC (Senior Courser)

Herding: HT (Herding Tested); PT (Pre-Trial Tested); HS (Herding Started); HI (Herding Intermediate); HX (Herding Excellent); HCh. (Herding Champion)

Tracking: TD (Tracking Dog); TDX (Tracking Dog Excellent)

Agility: NAD (Novice Agility); OAD (Open Agility); ADX (Agility Excellent); MAX (Master Agility)

Earthdog Tests: JE (Junior Earthdog); SE (Senior Earthdog); ME (Master Earthdog)

Canine Good Citizen: CGC

Combination: DC (Dual Champion—Ch. and Fch.); TC (Triple Champion—Ch., Fch., and OTCh.)

spaniels and pointing breeds only, are noncompetitive and are a means of judging the dog's ability as well as that of the handler.

Hunting is a very large and complex part of canine sports, and if you own one of the breeds that hunts, the events are a great treat for your dog and you. He gets to do what he was bred for, and you get to work with him and watch him do it. You'll be proud of and amazed at what your dog can do.

Fortunately, the AKC publishes a series of booklets on these events, which outline the rules and regulations and include a glossary of the sometimes complicated terms. The AKC also publishes newsletters for field trialers and hunting test enthusiasts. The United Kennel Club (UKC) also has informative materials for the hunter and his dog.

Retrievers and other sporting breeds get to do what they're bred to in hunting tests.

HERDING TESTS AND TRIALS

Herding, like hunting, dates back to the first known uses man made of dogs. The interest in herding today is widespread, and if you own a herding breed, you can join in the activity. Herding dogs are tested for their natural skills to keep a flock of ducks, sheep or cattle together. If your dog shows potential, you can start at the testing level, where your dog can earn a title for showing an inherent herding ability. With training you can advance to the trial level, where your dog should be capable of controlling even difficult livestock in diverse situations.

LURE COURSING

The AKC Tests and Trials for Lure Coursing are open to traditional sighthounds—Greyhounds, Whippets,

Borzoi, Salukis, Afghan Hounds, Ibizan Hounds and Scottish Deerhounds—as well as to Basenjis and Rhodesian Ridgebacks. Hounds are judged on overall ability, follow, speed, agility and endurance. This is possibly the most exciting of the trials for spectators, because the speed and agility of the dogs is awesome to watch as they chase the lure (or "course") in heats of two or three dogs at a time.

TRACKING

Tracking is another activity in which almost any dog can compete because every dog that sniffs the ground when taken outdoors is, in fact, tracking. The hard part comes when the rules as to what, when and where the dog tracks are determined by a person, not the dog! Tracking tests cover a large area of fields, woods and roads. The tracks are laid hours before the dogs go to work on them, and include "tricks" like cross-tracks and sharp turns. If you're interested in search-and-rescue work, this is the place to start.

This tracking dog is hot on the trail.

EARTHDOG TESTS FOR SMALL TERRIERS AND DACHSHUNDS

These tests are open to Australian, Bedlington, Border, Cairn, Dandie Dinmont, Smooth and Wire Fox, Lakeland, Norfolk, Norwich, Scottish, Sealyham, Skye, Welsh and West Highland White Terriers as well as Dachshunds. The dogs need no prior training for this terrier sport. There is a qualifying test on the day of the event, so dog and handler learn the rules on the spot. These tests, or "digs," sometimes end with informal races in the late afternoon.

Here are some of the extracurricular obedience and racing activities that are not regulated by the AKC or UKC, but are generally run by clubs or a group of dog fanciers and are often open to all.

Canine Freestyle This activity is something new on the scene and is variously likened to dancing, dressage or ice skating. It is meant to show the athleticism of the dog, but also requires showmanship on the part of the dog's handler. If you and your dog like to ham it up for friends, you might want to look into freestyle.

Lure coursing lets sighthounds do what they do best—run!

Scent Hurdle Racing Scent hurdle racing is purely a fun activity sponsored by obedience clubs with members forming competing teams. The height of the hurdles is based on the size of the shortest dog on the team. On a signal, one team dog is released on each of two side-by-side courses and must clear every hurdle before picking up its own dumbbell from a platform and returning over the jumps to the handler. As each dog returns, the next on that team is sent. Of course, that is what the dogs are supposed to do. When the dogs improvise (going under or around the hurdles, stealing another dog's dumbbell, and so forth), it no doubt frustrates the handlers, but just adds to the fun for everyone else.

Flyball This type of racing is similar, but after negotiating the four hurdles, the dog comes to a flyball box, steps on a lever that releases a tennis ball into the air, catches the ball and returns over the hurdles to the starting point. This game also becomes extremely fun for spectators because the dogs sometimes cheat by catching a ball released by the dog in the next lane. Three titles can be earned—Flyball Dog (F.D.), Flyball Dog Excellent (F.D.X.) and Flyball Dog Champion (Fb.D.Ch.)—all awarded by the North American Flyball Association, Inc.

Dogsledding The name conjures up the Rocky Mountains or the frigid North, but you can find dogsled clubs in such unlikely spots as Maryland, North Carolina and Virginia! Dogsledding is primarily for the Nordic breeds such as the Alaskan Malamutes, Siberian Huskies and Samoyeds, but other breeds can try. There are some practical backyard applications to this sport, too. With parental supervision, almost any strong dog could pull a child's sled.

Coming over the A-frame on an agility course.

These are just some of the many recreational ways you can get to know and understand your multifaceted dog better and have fun doing it.

chapter 10

Your Dog
and your
Family

by Bardi McLennan

Adding a dog automatically increases your family by one, no matter whether you live alone in an apartment or are part of a mother, father and six kids household. The single-person family is fair game for numerous and varied canine misconceptions as to who is dog and who pays the bills, whereas a dog in a houseful of children will consider himself to be just one of the gang, littermates all. One dog and one child may give a dog reason to believe they are both kids or both dogs.

Either interpretation requires parental supervision and sometimes speedy intervention.

As soon as one paw goes through the door into your home, Rufus (or Rufina) has to make many adjustments to become a part of your family. Your job is to make him fit in as painlessly as possible. An older dog may have some frame of reference from past experience, but to a 10-week-old puppy, everything is brand new: people, furniture, stairs, when and where people eat, sleep or watch TV, his own place and everyone else's space, smells, sounds, outdoors—everything!

Puppies, and newly acquired dogs of any age, do not need what we think of as "freedom." If you leave a new dog or puppy loose in the house, you will almost certainly return to chaotic destruction and the dog will forever after equate your homecoming with a time of punishment to be dreaded. It is unfair to give your dog what amounts to "freedom to get into trouble." Instead, confine him to a crate for brief periods of your absence (up to three or four hours) and, for the long haul, a workday for example, confine him to one untrashable area with his own toys, a bowl of water and a radio left on (low) in another room.

Lots of pets get along with each other just fine.

For the first few days, when not confined, put Rufus on a long leash tied to your wrist or waist. This umbilical cord method enables the dog to learn all about you from your body language and voice, and to learn by his own actions which things in the house are NO! and which ones are rewarded by "Good dog." Housetraining will be easier with the pup always by your side. Speaking of which, accidents do happen. That goal of "completely housetrained" takes up to a year, or the length of time it takes the pup to mature.

The All-Adult Family

Most dogs in an adults-only household today are likely to be latchkey pets, with no one home all day but the

dog. When you return after a tough day on the job, the
dog can and should be your relaxation therapy. But
going home can instead be a daily frustration.

Separation anxiety is a very common problem for the
dog in a working household. It may begin with whines
and barks of loneliness, but it will soon escalate into a
frenzied destruction derby. That is why it is so important to set aside the time to teach a dog to relax when
left alone in his confined area and to understand that
he can trust you to return.

Let the dog get used to your work schedule in easy
stages. Confine him to one room and go in and out of
that room over and over again. Be casual about it. No
physical, voice or eye contact. When the pup no longer
even notices your comings and goings, leave the house
for varying lengths of time, returning to stay home for
a few minutes and gradually increasing the time away.
This training can take days, but the dog is learning that
you haven't left him forever and that he can trust you.

Any time you leave the dog, but especially during this
training period, be casual about your departure. No
anxiety-building fond farewells. Just "Bye" and go!
Remember the "Good dog" when you return to find
everything more or less as you left it.

If things are a mess (or even a disaster) when you
return, greet the dog, take him outside to eliminate,
and then put him in his crate while you clean up. Rant
and rave in the shower! *Do not* punish the dog. You
were not there when it happened, and the rule is: Only
punish as you catch the dog in the act of wrongdoing.
Obviously, it makes sense to get your latchkey puppy
when you'll have a week or two to spend on these training essentials.

Family weekend activities should include Rufus whenever possible. Depending on the pup's age, now is the
time for a long walk in the park, playtime in the backyard, a hike in the woods. Socializing is as important as
health care, good food and physical exercise, so visiting Aunt Emma or Uncle Harry and the next-door

neighbor's dog or cat is essential to developing an outgoing, friendly temperament in your pet.

If you are a single adult, socializing Rufus at home and away will prevent him from becoming overly protective of you (or just overly attached) and will also prevent such behavioral problems as dominance or fear of strangers.

Babies

Whether already here or on the way, babies figure larger than life in the eyes of a dog. If the dog is there first, let him in on all your baby preparations in the house. When baby arrives, let Rufus sniff any item of clothing that has been on the baby before Junior comes home. Then let Mom greet the dog first before introducing the new family member. Hold the baby down for the dog to see and sniff, but make sure someone's holding the dog on lead in case of any sudden moves. Don't play keep-away or tease the dog with the baby, which only invites undesirable jumping up.

The dog and the baby are "family," and for starters can be treated almost as equals. Things rapidly change, however, especially when baby takes to creeping around on all fours on the dog's turf or, better yet, has yummy pudding all over her face and hands! That's when a lot of things in the dog's and baby's lives become more separate than equal.

Dogs are perfect confidants.

Toddlers make terrible dog owners, but if you can't avoid the combination, use patient discipline (that is, positive teaching rather than punishment), and use time-outs before you run out of patience.

139

A dog and a baby (or toddler, or an assertive young child) should never be left alone together. Take the dog with you or confine him. With a baby or youngsters in the house, you'll have plenty of use for that wonderful canine safety device called a crate!

Young Children

Any dog in a house with kids will behave pretty much as the kids do, good or bad. But even good dogs and good children can get into trouble when play becomes rowdy and active.

Teach children how to play nicely with a puppy.

Legs bobbing up and down, shrill voices screeching, a ball hurtling overhead, all add up to exuberant frustration for a dog who's just trying to be part of the gang. In a pack of puppies, any legs or toys being chased would be caught by a set of teeth, and all the pups involved would understand that is how the game is played. Kids do not understand this, nor do parents tolerate it. Bring Rufus indoors before you have reason to regret it. This is time-out, not a punishment.

You can explain the situation to the children and tell them they must play quieter games until the puppy learns not to grab them with his mouth. Unfortunately, you can't explain it that easily to the dog. With adult supervision, they will learn how to play together.

Young children love to tease. Sticking their faces or wiggling their hands or fingers in the dog's face is teasing. To another person it might be just annoying, but it is threatening to a dog. There's another difference: We can make the child stop by an explanation, but the only way a dog can stop it is with a warning growl and then with teeth. Teasing is the major cause of children being bitten by their pets. Treat it seriously.

140

Older Children

The best age for a child to get a first dog is between the ages of 8 and 12. That's when kids are able to accept some real responsibility for their pet. Even so, take the child's vow of "I will never *ever* forget to feed (brush, walk, etc.) the dog" for what it's worth: a child's good intention at that moment. Most kids today have extra lessons, soccer practice, Little League, ballet, and so forth piled on top of school schedules. There will be many times when Mom will have to come to the dog's rescue. "I walked the dog for you so you can set the table for me" is one way to get around a missed appointment without laying on blame or guilt.

Kids in this age group make excellent obedience trainers because they are into the teaching/learning process themselves and they lack the self-consciousness of adults. Attending a dog show is something the whole family can enjoy, and watching Junior Showmanship may catch the eye of the kids. Older children can begin to get involved in many of the recreational activities that were reviewed in the previous chapter. Some of the agility obstacles, for example, can be set up in the backyard as a family project (with an adult making sure all the equipment is safe and secure for the dog).

Older kids are also beginning to look to the future, and may envision themselves as veterinarians or trainers or show dog handlers or writers of the next Lassie best-seller. Dogs are perfect confidants for these dreams. They won't tell a soul.

Other Pets

Introduce all pets tactfully. In a dog/cat situation, hold the dog, not the cat. Let two dogs meet on neutral turf—a stroll in the park or a walk down the street—with both on loose leads to permit all the normal canine ways of saying hello, including routine sniffing, circling, more sniffing, and so on. Small creatures such as hamsters, chinchillas or mice must be kept safe from their natural predators (dogs and cats).

Festive Family Occasions

Parties are great for people, but not necessarily for puppies. Until all the guests have arrived, put the dog in his crate or in a room where he won't be disturbed. A socialized dog can join the fun later as long as he's not underfoot, annoying guests or into the hors d'oeuvres.

There are a few dangers to consider, too. Doors opening and closing can allow a puppy to slip out unnoticed in the confusion, and you'll be organizing a search party instead of playing host or hostess. Party food and buffet service are not for dogs. Let Rufus party in his crate with a nice big dog biscuit.

At Christmas time, not only are tree decorations dangerous and breakable (and perhaps family heirlooms), but extreme caution should be taken with the lights, cords and outlets for the tree lights and any other festive lighting. Occasionally a dog lifts a leg, ignoring the fact that the tree is indoors. To avoid this, use a canine repellent, made for gardens, on the tree. Or keep him out of the tree room unless supervised. And whatever you do, *don't* invite trouble by hanging his toys on the tree!

Car Travel

Before you plan a vacation by car or RV with Rufus, be sure he enjoys car travel. Nothing spoils a holiday quicker than a carsick dog! Work within the dog's comfort level. Get in the car with the dog in his crate or attached to a canine car safety belt and just sit there until he relaxes. That's all. Next time, get in the car, turn on the engine and go nowhere. Just sit. When that is okay, turn on the engine and go around the block. Now you can go for a ride and include a stop where you get out, leaving the dog for a minute or two.

On a warm day, always park in the shade and leave windows open several inches. And return quickly. It only takes 10 minutes for a car to become an overheated steel death trap.

Motel or Pet Motel?

Not all motels or hotels accept pets, but you have a much better choice today than even a few years ago. To find a dog-friendly lodging, look at *On the Road Again With Man's Best Friend*, a series of directories that detail bed and breakfasts, inns, family resorts and other hotels/motels. Some places require a refundable deposit to cover any damage incurred by the dog. More B&Bs accept pets now, but some restrict the size.

If taking Rufus with you is not feasible, check out boarding kennels in your area. Your veterinarian may offer this service, or recommend a kennel or two he or she is familiar with. Go see the facilities for yourself, ask about exercise, diet, housing, and so on. Or, if you'd rather have Rufus stay home, look into bonded petsitters, many of whom will also bring in the mail and water your plants.

chapter 11

Your Dog
and your
Community

by Bardi McLennan

Step outside your home with your dog and you are no longer just family, you are both part of your community. This is when the phrase "responsible pet ownership" takes on serious implications. For starters, it means you pick up after your dog—not just occasionally, but every time your dog eliminates away from home. That means you have joined the Plastic Baggy Brigade! You always have plastic sandwich bags in your pocket and several in the car. It means you teach your kids how to use them, too. If you think this is "yucky," just imagine what

the person (a non-doggy person) who inadvertently steps in the mess thinks!

144

Your responsibility extends to your neighbors: To their ears (no annoying barking); to their property (their garbage, their lawn, their flower beds, their cat—especially their cat); to their kids (on bikes, at play); to their kids' toys and sports equipment.

There are numerous dog-related laws, ranging from simple dog licensing and leash laws to those holding you liable for any physical injury or property damage done by your dog. These laws are in place to protect everyone in the community, including you and your dog. There are town ordinances and state laws which are by no means the same in all towns or all states. Ignorance of the law won't get you off the hook. The time to find out what the laws are where you live is now.

Be sure your dog's license is current. This is not just a good local ordinance, it can make the difference between finding your lost dog or not.

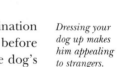

Dressing your dog up makes him appealing to strangers.

Many states now require proof of rabies vaccination and that the dog has been spayed or neutered before issuing a license. At the same time, keep up the dog's annual immunizations.

Never let your dog run loose in the neighborhood. This will not only keep you on the right side of the leash law, it's the outdoor version of the rule about not giving your dog "freedom to get into trouble."

Good Canine Citizen

Sometimes it's hard for a dog's owner to assess whether or not the dog is sufficiently socialized to be accepted by the community at large. Does Rufus or Rufina display good, controlled behavior in public? The AKC's Canine Good Citizen program is available through many dog organizations. If your dog passes the test, the title "CGC" is earned.

The overall purpose is to turn your dog into a good neighbor and to teach you about your responsibility to your community as a dog owner. Here are the ten things your dog must do willingly:

1. Accept a stranger stopping to chat with you.
2. Sit and be petted by a stranger.
3. Allow a stranger to handle him or her as a groomer or veterinarian would.
4. Walk nicely on a loose lead.
5. Walk calmly through a crowd.
6. Sit and down on command, then stay in a sit or down position while you walk away.
7. Come when called.
8. Casually greet another dog.
9. React confidently to distractions.
10. Accept being left alone with someone other than you and not become overly agitated or nervous.

Schools and Dogs

Schools are getting involved with pet ownership on an educational level. It has been proven that children who are kind to animals are humane in their attitude toward other people as adults.

A dog is a child's best friend, and so children are often primary pet owners, if not the primary caregivers. Unfortunately, they are also the ones most often bitten by dogs. This occurs due to a lack of understanding that pets, no matter how sweet, cuddly and loving, are still animals. Schools, along with parents, dog clubs, dog fanciers and the AKC, are working to change all that with video programs for children not only in grade school, but in the nursery school and pre-kindergarten age group. Teaching youngsters how to be responsible dog owners is important community work. When your dog has a CGC, volunteer to take part in an educational classroom event put on by your dog club.

Boy Scout Merit Badge

A Merit Badge for Dog Care can be earned by any Boy Scout ages 11 to 18. The requirements are not easy, but amount to a complete course in responsible dog care and general ownership. Here are just a few of the things a Scout must do to earn that badge:

Point out ten parts of the dog using the correct names.

Give a report (signed by parent or guardian) on your care of the dog (feeding, food used, housing, exercising, grooming and bathing), plus what has been done to keep the dog healthy.

Explain the right way to obedience train a dog, and demonstrate three comments.

Several of the requirements have to do with health care, including first aid, handling a hurt dog, and the dangers of home treatment for a serious ailment.

The final requirement is to know the local laws and ordinances involving dogs.

There are similar programs for Girl Scouts and 4-H members.

Local Clubs

Local dog clubs are no longer in existence just to put on a yearly dog show. Today, they are apt to be the hub of the community's involvement with pets. Dog clubs conduct educational forums with big-name speakers, stage demonstrations of canine talent in a busy mall and take dogs of various breeds to schools for classroom discussion.

The quickest way to feel accepted as a member in a club is to volunteer your services! Offer to help with something—anything—and watch your popularity (and your interest) grow.

Therapy Dogs

Once your dog has earned that essential CGC and reliably demonstrates a steady, calm temperament, you could look into what therapy dogs are doing in your area.

Therapy dogs go with their owners to visit patients at hospitals or nursing homes, generally remaining on leash but able to coax a pat from a stiffened hand, a smile from a blank face, a few words from sealed lips or a hug from someone in need of love.

Nursing homes cover a wide range of patient care. Some specialize in care of the elderly, some in the treatment of specific illnesses, some in physical therapy. Children's facilities also welcome visits from trained therapy dogs for boosting morale in their pediatric patients. Hospice care for the terminally ill and the at-home care of AIDS patients are other areas where this canine visiting is desperately needed. Therapy dog training comes first.

Your dog can make a difference in lots of lives.

There is a lot more involved than just taking your nice friendly pooch to someone's bedside. Doing therapy dog work involves your own emotional stability as well as that of your dog. But once you have met all the requirements for this work, making the rounds once a week or once a month with your therapy dog is possibly the most rewarding of all community activities.

Disaster Aid

This community service is definitely not for everyone, partly because it is time-consuming. The initial training is rigorous, and there can be no let-up in the continuing workouts, because members are on call 24 hours a day to go wherever they are needed at a moment's notice. But if you think you would like to be able to assist in a disaster, look into search-and-rescue work. The network of search-and-rescue volunteers is worldwide, and all members of the American Rescue Dog Association (ARDA) who are qualified to do this work are volunteers who train and maintain their own dogs.

Physical Aid

Most people are familiar with Seeing Eye dogs, which serve as blind people's eyes, but not with all the other work that dogs are trained to do to assist the disabled. Dogs are also specially trained to pull wheelchairs, carry school books, pick up dropped objects, open and close doors. Some also are ears for the deaf. All these assistance-trained dogs, by the way, are allowed anywhere "No Pet" signs exist (as are therapy dogs when properly identified). Getting started in any of this fascinating work requires a background in dog training and canine behavior, but there are also volunteer jobs ranging from answering the phone to cleaning out kennels to providing a foster home for a puppy. You have only to ask.

Making the rounds with your therapy dog can be very rewarding.

Beyond

the

Basics

part four

chapter 12

Recommended Reading

Books

ABOUT HEALTH CARE

Ackerman, Lowell. *Guide to Skin and Haircoat Problems in Dogs.* Loveland, Colo.: Alpine Publications, 1994.

Alderton, David. *The Dog Care Manual.* Hauppauge, N.Y.: Barron's Educational Series, Inc., 1986.

American Kennel Club. *American Kennel Club Dog Care and Training.* New York: Howell Book House, 1991.

Bamberger, Michelle, DVM. *Help! The Quick Guide to First Aid for Your Dog.* New York: Howell Book House, 1995.

Carlson, Delbert, DVM, and James Giffin, MD. *Dog Owner's Home Veterinary Handbook.* New York: Howell Book House, 1992.

DeBitetto, James, DVM, and Sarah Hodgson. *You & Your Puppy.* New York: Howell Book House, 1995.

Humphries, Jim, DVM. *Dr. Jim's Animal Clinic for Dogs.* New York: Howell Book House, 1994.

McGinnis, Terri. *The Well Dog Book.* New York: Random House, 1991.

Pitcairn, Richard and Susan. *Natural Health for Dogs.* Emmaus, Pa.: Rodale Press, 1982.

ABOUT DOG SHOWS

Hall, Lynn. *Dog Showing for Beginners.* New York: Howell Book House, 1994.

Nichols, Virginia Tuck. *How to Show Your Own Dog.* Neptune, N. J.: TFH, 1970.

Vanacore, Connie. *Dog Showing, An Owner's Guide.* New York: Howell Book House, 1990.

ABOUT TRAINING

Ammen, Amy. *Training in No Time*. New York: Howell Book House, 1995.

Baer, Ted. *Communicating With Your Dog*. Hauppauge, N.Y.: Barron's Educational Series, Inc., 1989.

Benjamin, Carol Lea. *Dog Problems*. New York: Howell Book House, 1989.

Benjamin, Carol Lea. *Dog Training for Kids*. New York: Howell Book House, 1988.

Benjamin, Carol Lea. *Mother Knows Best*. New York: Howell Book House, 1985.

Benjamin, Carol Lea. *Surviving Your Dog's Adolescence*. New York: Howell Book House, 1993.

Bohnenkamp, Gwen. *Manners for the Modern Dog*. San Francisco: Perfect Paws, 1990.

Dibra, Bashkim. *Dog Training by Bash*. New York: Dell, 1992.

Dunbar, Ian, PhD, MRCVS. *Dr. Dunbar's Good Little Dog Book*, James & Kenneth Publishers, 2140 Shattuck Ave. #2406, Berkeley, Calif. 94704. (510) 658–8588. Order from the publisher.

Dunbar, Ian, PhD, MRCVS. *How to Teach a New Dog Old Tricks*, James & Kenneth Publishers. Order from the publisher; address above.

Dunbar, Ian, PhD, MRCVS, and Gwen Bohnenkamp. Booklets on *Preventing Aggression; Housetraining; Chewing; Digging; Barking; Socialization; Fearfulness; and Fighting*, James & Kenneth Publishers. Order from the publisher; address above.

Evans, Job Michael. *People, Pooches and Problems*. New York: Howell Book House, 1991.

Kilcommons, Brian and Sarah Wilson. *Good Owners, Great Dogs*. New York: Warner Books, 1992.

McMains, Joel M. *Dog Logic—Companion Obedience*. New York: Howell Book House, 1992.

Rutherford, Clarice and David H. Neil, MRCVS. *How to Raise a Puppy You Can Live With*. Loveland, Colo.: Alpine Publications, 1982.

Volhard, Jack and Melissa Bartlett. *What All Good Dogs Should Know: The Sensible Way to Train*. New York: Howell Book House, 1991.

ABOUT BREEDING

Harris, Beth J. Finder. *Breeding a Litter, The Complete Book of Prenatal and Postnatal Care*. New York: Howell Book House, 1983.

Holst, Phyllis, DVM. *Canine Reproduction*. Loveland, Colo.: Alpine Publications, 1985.

Walkowicz, Chris and Bonnie Wilcox, DVM. *Successful Dog Breeding, The Complete Handbook of Canine Midwifery.* New York: Howell Book House, 1994.

ABOUT ACTIVITIES

American Rescue Dog Association. *Search and Rescue Dogs.* New York: Howell Book House, 1991.

Barwig, Susan and Stewart Hilliard. *Schutzhund.* New York: Howell Book House, 1991.

Beaman, Arthur S. *Lure Coursing.* New York: Howell Book House, 1994.

Daniels, Julie. *Enjoying Dog Agility—From Backyard to Competition.* New York: Doral Publishing, 1990.

Davis, Kathy Diamond. *Therapy Dogs.* New York: Howell Book House, 1992.

Gallup, Davis Anne. *Running With Man's Best Friend.* Loveland, Colo.: Alpine Publications, 1986.

Habgood, Dawn and Robert. *On the Road Again With Man's Best Friend.* New England, Mid-Atlantic, West Coast and Southeast editions. Selective guides to area bed and breakfasts, inns, hotels and resorts that welcome guests and their dogs. New York: Howell Book House, 1995.

Holland, Vergil S. *Herding Dogs.* New York: Howell Book House, 1994.

LaBelle, Charlene G. *Backpacking With Your Dog.* Loveland, Colo.: Alpine Publications, 1993.

Simmons-Moake, Jane. *Agility Training, The Fun Sport for All Dogs.* New York: Howell Book House, 1991.

Spencer, James B. *Hup! Training Flushing Spaniels the American Way.* New York: Howell Book House, 1992.

Spencer, James B. *Point! Training the All-Seasons Birddog.* New York: Howell Book House, 1995.

Tarrant, Bill. *Training the Hunting Retriever.* New York: Howell Book House, 1991.

Volhard, Jack and Wendy. *The Canine Good Citizen.* New York: Howell Book House, 1994.

General Titles

Haggerty, Captain Arthur J. *How to Get Your Pet Into Show Business.* New York: Howell Book House, 1994.

McLennan, Bardi. *Dogs and Kids, Parenting Tips.* New York: Howell Book House, 1993.

Moran, Patti J. *Pet Sitting for Profit, A Complete Manual for Professional Success.* New York: Howell Book House, 1992.

Scalisi, Danny and Libby Moses. *When Rover Just Won't Do, Over 2,000 Suggestions for Naming Your Dog.* New York: Howell Book House, 1993.

Sife, Wallace, PhD. *The Loss of a Pet.* New York: Howell Book House, 1993.

Wrede, Barbara J. *Civilizing Your Puppy.* Hauppauge, N.Y.: Barron's Educational Series, 1992.

Magazines

The AKC GAZETTE, The Official Journal for the Sport of Purebred Dogs. American Kennel Club, 51 Madison Ave., New York, NY.

Bloodlines Journal. United Kennel Club, 100 E. Kilgore Rd., Kalamazoo, MI.

Dog Fancy. Fancy Publications, 3 Burroughs, Irvine, CA 92718

Dog World. Maclean Hunter Publishing Corp., 29 N. Wacker Dr., Chicago, IL 60606.

Videos

"SIRIUS Puppy Training," by Ian Dunbar, PhD, MRCVS. James & Kenneth Publishers, 2140 Shattuck Ave. #2406, Berkeley, CA 94704. Order from the publisher.

"Training the Companion Dog," from Dr. Dunbar's British TV Series, James & Kenneth Publishers. (See address above).

The American Kennel Club produces videos on every breed of dog, as well as on hunting tests, field trials and other areas of interest to purebred dog owners. For more information, write to AKC/Video Fulfillment, 5580 Centerview Dr., Suite 200, Raleigh, NC 27606.

chapter 13

Resources

Breed Clubs

Every breed recognized by the American Kennel Club has a national (parent) club. National clubs are a great source of information on your breed. You can get the name of the secretary of the club by contacting:

The American Kennel Club
51 Madison Avenue
New York, NY 10010
(212) 696-8200

There are also numerous all-breed, individual breed, obedience, hunting and other special-interest dog clubs across the country. The American Kennel Club can provide you with a geographical list of clubs to find ones in your area. Contact them at the above address.

Registry Organizations

Registry organizations register purebred dogs. The American Kennel Club is the oldest and largest in this country, and currently recognizes over 130 breeds. The United Kennel Club registers some breeds the AKC doesn't (including the American Pit Bull Terrier and the Miniature Fox Terrier) as well as many of the same breeds. The others included here are for your reference; the AKC can provide you with a list of foreign registries.

American Kennel Club
51 Madison Avenue
New York, NY 10010

United Kennel Club (UKC)
100 E. Kilgore Road
Kalamazoo, MI 49001-5598

American Dog Breeders Assn.
P.O. Box 1771
Salt Lake City, UT 84110
(Registers American Pit Bull Terriers)

Canadian Kennel Club
89 Skyway Avenue
Etobicoke, Ontario
Canada M9W 6R4

National Stock Dog Registry
P.O. Box 402
Butler, IN 46721
(Registers working stock dogs)

Orthopedic Foundation for Animals (OFA)
2300 E. Nifong Blvd.
Columbia, MO 65201-3856
(Hip registry)

Activity Clubs

Write to these organizations for information on the
activities they sponsor.

American Kennel Club
51 Madison Avenue
New York, NY 10010
(Conformation Shows, Obedience Trials, Field
Trials and Hunting Tests, Agility, Canine Good

Citizen, Lure Coursing, Herding, Tracking,
Earthdog Tests, Coonhunting.)

United Kennel Club
100 E. Kilgore Road
Kalamazoo, MI 49001-5598
(Conformation Shows, Obedience Trials, Agility,
Hunting for Various Breeds, Terrier Trials and
more.)

North American Flyball Assn.
1342 Jeff St.
Ypsilanti, MI 48198

International Sled Dog Racing Assn.
P.O. Box 446
Norman, ID 83848-0446

North American Working Dog Assn., Inc.
Southeast Kreisgruppe
P.O. Box 833
Brunswick, GA 31521

Trainers

Association of Pet Dog Trainers
P.O. Box 385
Davis, CA 95617
(800) PET–DOGS

American Dog Trainers' Network
161 West 4th St.
New York, NY 10014
(212) 727–7257

**National Association of Dog Obedience
Instructors**
2286 East Steel Rd.
St. Johns, MI 48879

Associations

American Dog Owners Assn.
1654 Columbia Tpk.
Castleton, NY 12033
(Combats anti-dog legislation)

Delta Society
P.O. Box 1080
Renton, WA 98057-1080
(Promotes the human/animal bond through
pet-assisted therapy and other programs)

Dog Writers Assn. of America (DWAA)
Sally Cooper, Secy.
222 Woodchuck Ln.
Harwinton, CT 06791

National Assn. for Search and Rescue (NASAR)
P.O. Box 3709
Fairfax, VA 22038

Therapy Dogs International
6 Hilltop Road
Mendham, NJ 07945